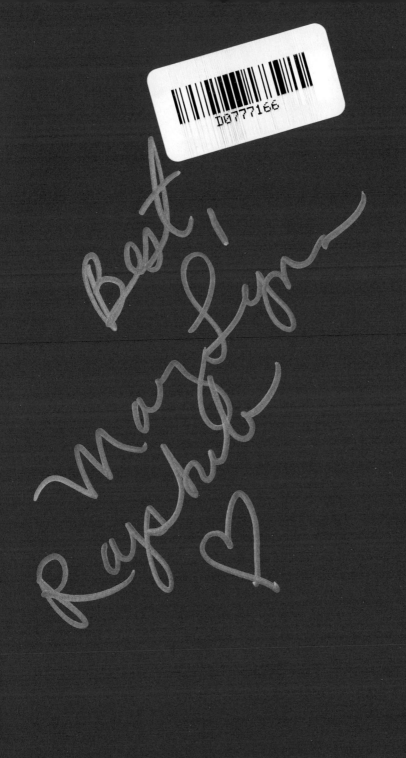

Best,

Mary Lynn

Raphele ♡

# FAME-ISH

*My Life at the
Edge of Stardom*

## MARY LYNN RAJSKUB

ABRAMS PRESS, NEW YORK

Library of Congress Control Number: 2021949383

ISBN: 978–1-4197–5479–1
eISBN: 978–1-64700–299–2

Printed and bound in the United States

10 9 8 7 6 5 4 3 2 1

Abrams books are available at special discounts when purchased in quantity for premiums
and promotions as well as fundraising or educational use. Special editions can also be created
to specification. For details, contact specialsales@abramsbooks.com or the address below.

Abrams Press® is a registered trademark of Harry N. Abrams, Inc.

**ABRAMS** The Art of Books
195 Broadway, New York, NY 10007
abramsbooks.com

# INTRODUCTION

*Things have really changed,* I thought as I drove my parents' Ford Explorer down Allen Road in Trenton, Michigan, in 2014. My mother had a sweatshirt made that read, I'M CHLOE O'BRIAN'S MOM!, in reference to the character I played on the wildly popular show *24.* She wanted the world to know. I had been on *Late Show with David Letterman* and in *GQ,* had visited the White House, and *People* listed me as "One of the World's Most Beautiful People." I had worked with tons of famous people and been in many TV shows and movies. I had made it!

Fifteen years prior, when I first started acting on TV, I remember my sister telling the cashier at Kroger, "She's famous!" I was mortified.

The cashier stared at us, like, *What the fuck are you talking about?*

"Don't you recognize her?"

"No."

My sister put the cashier in her place. "She's on *Veronica's Closet* on NBC!"

I wanted to disappear into an automatic trap door in the floor. This isn't how I was supposed to feel. I should be like James Brown or Tom Jones, diamonds on all my fingers, women throwing their underwear at me, "Hi, it's so nice for you to meet me." I'd bow, in my cape and platform shoes, and do a superstar shimmy. "Get up off that thang! Watch out, pussycat!" I'd say. Instead, I looked down and said nothing.

"If you don't know who she is, it's your loss!" Then my sister Kathy cascaded out with an air of superiority as I mouthed, "I'm sorry" to the cashier.

*Veronica's Closet* was Kirstie Alley's sitcom. She was coming in hot, off her star-making turn on *Cheers* as the will-they-or-won't-they love interest to Sam Malone. She played the owner of a lingerie shop. I was the androgynous love interest to her assistant, who was a closeted gay man. Progressive story line!

My family wanted to make sure that Trenton knew who I was. I signed a headshot that hangs in Del's Pizzeria, which I have been going to since I was a baby. Everyone was extra proud because where I grew up, people don't leave. Except my other sister who moved to Arizona, and she never heard the end of it. I got a bit of a pass because I got to be in Hollywood, baby! But still, every visit is punctuated with family members asking, "When are you visiting again?" "I'm here right now . . ." The truth is, it's not really my home anymore. When I'm there, it is peaceful, but soon I'm ready to go again.

When I was sixteen and new to driving, I remember passing this intersection heading toward the freeway into the great big world out there (which meant downtown Detroit). I would pass Kmart, White Castle, and the truck stop. The truck stop was a place I imagined hanging out in. What if I became a trucker? I could see the world. I'd imagine myself at the counter with a coffee, grizzled and wise.

I got the courage to walk in and the actuality of it was depressing and possibly dangerous. They saw me coming from the parking lot in my long-sleeve red Coca-Cola shirt with the white collar and my permed, short hair with the Brian Setzer curl on the middle of my forehead. When I walked through the front door, two truckers, a waitress, and a short-order cook stared at me. I had breached a sacred border; I wasn't allowed in here. I turned around and walked out. Like an American in Europe, I stuck out like a sore thumb. Those midwestern middle-age male truckers couldn't be further removed from the tiny wish of my sixteen-year-old angst-ridden heart. Just like that, my dream of being a trucker was dashed.

Luckily, acting was another way to escape and dream. My theater class was the only thing I liked in high school. Pretending to be someone else was also a means of survival. Being other people in plays and scenes was a way for me to experience emotions, impulses, and desires that I wasn't allowed to indulge in in my real life. If I let my true feelings out, it was just an invitation to be dismissed or hurt. I wasn't about to take that chance. Without acting, I was invisible. I practiced keeping what I wanted and who I was a secret. I would let friends in, or sometimes try with the boys I dated. But the only time I had a sense of full expression was when I was in character. That's when I was free to let loose and be vulnerable. Very pragmatic of me. I never imagined this coping mechanism would turn into a career. My small steps toward joy, my small wishes became dreams beyond anything I could have hoped for. I never imagined visiting California, let alone making a home and a life there.

In 2014, I was back in Trenton, wearing my dad's fleece coat and my mom's hat and gloves (like the queen I am) because I refused to invest in winter clothes, on my way to the new Applebee's. A Target had replaced the Kmart, and there was now a Panera Bread and an LA Fitness—developments at my home intersection. I settled into a crowded Applebee's, by myself.

"I'll have a sparkling water, please." The high school–age server scared me.

"We don't have that."

"OK . . ."

"Sorry, we ain't that fancy."

"No, that's OK!" I said a little too brightly. "I'll have a tonic water."

"What?"

"A tonic water?" She made a face to show that this request disgusted her. "A plain tonic water from the bar? Is that what you're talking about?"

"Yeah, from the gun. Just . . ." I acted out spraying the gun and made its sound. I'm really good at space work, it's part of being an improviser.

"We have Coke and Sprite."

"That's OK. The tonic water will be fine."

"You look like this actress . . ."

"Oh really? That's cool . . ." I demure.

"There's this actress that looks like you, do you know who I'm talking about?" She couldn't believe the resemblance.

"Hmm, Angelina Jolie? I get that sometimes . . ."

The server laughs way too hard. "No! Of course not. You're *funny*," she said, in a way to let me know I was not funny.

"*Girl Interrupted* Angelina Jolie, you know, drinking tonic water, wearing her dad's fleece?!"

She was done with me. "No. That's not it." She left me in peace.

A little later, when I was nearing the end of my southwestern grilled chicken quesadilla salad, employees began to pass my table, one by one, pretending not to stare. Some tried to be useful. "Are you sure you don't want a refill on that?" They back away, giggling, and run over to a busboy and another server to huddle over a phone, google me, and compare online pictures to the real thing. By the time I paid for the check, they knew they had the real deal.

As I was leaving the host called after me. "Excuse me, can I ask you a question?"

"OK."

"You're not Mary Lynn Rajskub are you?"

"Yeah, I am."

The hostess turns to her coworker. "I told you!"

I stand there.

"I knew it was you, she didn't believe me! Why are you here?"

"Visiting my family."

"We love Gail the Snail. Can we get a picture with you? Hold on." She grabs a saltshaker. (My character on *It's Always Sunny in Philadelphia* gets salt thrown at her to try and make her go away.) "OMG, can we throw salt on you for the picture?!"

"Um . . ."

The hostess has already positioned her camera for a selfie while the other one photobombs and throws salt. "Please!"

They needed to take about fifteen pictures, to get the right look, and so you could actually see salt flying in the air. They finally start to calm down, like after a good romp in the hay.

I give a strained smile, wiping salt off my face. "You got it?"

They were already walking away from me. "Thanks! Have a good time in Michigan!"

"I'll try! I actually have salt in my eye now."

"I can't believe that's her!" said one to the other.

It happens on Twitter too. "I can't believe she responded to me!" wrote Birdlover4lyfe42, after he tagged me in a tweet.

"I can hear you and see you, I'm right here!" I tweeted at him. I'm not J.Lo, of course I saw your comment. I see all your comments. I'm in that sweet spot of fame, where sometimes people are literally shaking when they meet me, and other times they're heckling me at a stand-up show.

The first time I tried to write, it was a similar process. I started by writing about being on TV and making jokes about the weather, being silly and sarcastic. My inner heckler came out. This really big, scary, high guy inside me yelled, "No one cares! You're not smart enough to write a book!" *Please be quiet, I'm writing a book.* "Sit down and write it then! Good luck," my inner heckler said.

I called my agent at the time, who sent me to the book department at my agency. His name was Tony and he was a huge fan of mine. He wanted me to know he has seen me at a club I frequently performed at, called Largo. He told me on the phone about all the music he liked and concerts he had been to. He said it was going to be great and he'd be happy to help me every step of the way with my book. We had several meetings, most of which was him talking and me listening. He told me how talented he thought my boyfriend was (I was dating a composer who worked with Paul Thomas Anderson). I would leave the meetings exhausted and go home to labor over the pages for my book proposal, all of which seemed to come up flat.

Ten years later, with more life experience, and having developed a TV script of my own, not to mention many more sets of stand-up comedy under my belt (which means performing original material), I started to write again. This time I had real confidence and a support system. I was still silly and sarcastic, but as I continued to write, something way more sinister started to emerge: my actual thoughts and feelings! It turned out I was a real person with insights and a certain perspective on the world. This is a whole new part of my life that I didn't know about until fifty years into living. Now I can't shut up!

In this book, you'll find tales from my relationships, interactions with my neighbors, job triumphs and letdowns, and all the insight and humor that comes with it. It turns out, after fifty years of living, I was able to shut down my inner heckler and let the book come out. I hope you enjoy reading it as much as I enjoyed writing it.

# INTERNATIONAL SUPERSTAR

I like being recognized from your favorite movies and TV shows. *It's Always Sunny in Philadelphia, Brooklyn Nine-Nine, Mr. Show with Bob and David, Punch-Drunk Love, Sweet Home Alabama,* and *Veronica's Closet* (from the nineties, come on guys). You get it. I have a lot of credits. I am an international superstar. It's not easy carrying that kind of glory around. No matter what people throw at me, I gotta be ready.

"Do I know you?"

"Yeah, it's from TV."

"No, that's not it.

"Yes, it is! I'm an international superstar."

"I know! It's from carpool!"

"No, I don't even live in this school district."

"You look like someone who might be on *Parks and Rec.*"

"That's not even a person. That's an amalgamation of multiple people in your head. I'll take it, I'll take it. Thank you." It doesn't matter to me that they don't know me or my work. I might as well be Jenna Fischer. (We are interchangeable, right?)

Sometimes people believe I'm Jenna Fischer. Especially if I have my glasses on. I'm not. Just to be clear I'm not the girl from *The Office*, although I did sign her headshot once, "All my love, Jenna." I tweeted her after like, "Oh hey girl! Holding it down over here! Doing the good work!" She did not respond.

A lot of people recognize me from the hugely popular TV show *24*. It's a drama. It was a long time ago but it still airs in Africa. (African guys on Twitter love me.) What's that? You've never heard of it? It is only one of the most influential, groundbreaking dramas to be on network TV. It single-handedly changed the landscape of television with its fast-paced plot and cliff-hangers. It was the first binged-watched show before "binge-watch" was a term.

I was on this show for six to nine years (I have a very bad memory and sense of time). I played a computer genius named Chloe O'Brian who could save the world from a terrorist attack using only her computer. I can't really do that. I just want you to know that for the record, in case anyone out there wants me to fix their computer or disarm a nuclear bomb.

Also, I wasn't even really typing on the show. Shit would be hitting the fan and my character would say, "I'm on it. Copy that." and I would start typing some high-level intelligent stuff. In reality, I was just typing positive affirmations to myself. "Downloading facial recognition software now!" *Mary Lynn, you are doing a great job. Don't take Kiefer's intensity so personally, he's just busy acting right now.* The other actors would walk by hoping to see the hacked government files and they would just see *You are a divine child of God. Love and light surround you, always. Rainbows and unicorns.*

The show starred Kiefer Sutherland as federal agent Jack Bauer, a guy with a moral code to save people who are in danger, even if it goes against protocol. It was not unusual to find Jack torturing terrorists and their associates in order to get information. I was his go-to gal. I guided him down many hallways, instructed him to "toggle left!" helping to dismantle bombs and of course get in and out of places where a high-security breach was involved. I always had his back. My character was a rule follower and a government employee, but I would do anything Jack needed me to. Many times, people have told me that watching *24* helped them during a hard period in their lives. Soldiers in Iraq were big fans. A few people told me they watched the show while they were recovering from surgeries. Couples, families, and friends bonded over it and have remained dedicated fans. People on both sides of politics loved the show. I miss those days. I had a paycheck and a purpose.

I walked right into the part of a lifetime. *24* was already a huge hit. I breezed on as a nerdy, caustic computer genius. The creator of the show, Joel Surnow, had seen me in a Paul Thomas Anderson movie called *Punch-Drunk Love*, where I played a bitchy overbearing sister to Adam Sandler's character, and said, "I like that. I want to write a part for you." Just that meeting could have kept me going for a couple of years. As an actor, any type of acknowledgment or positive feedback is a big cue to keep going. So it was already enough that he said he wanted to write a part for me. The fact that he did, blew the lid off. I wasn't meant to work more than a few episodes, but something clicked. On a dry, dramatic show, my character became a source of levity. I had only done comedy and didn't know if I could do drama. I had faith in myself, but certainly had no idea how to fit in on this show. It turns out I didn't fit in and it worked. I learned on the job how to be a dramatic actress on television. I was trained on how to be on a red carpet and how to give interviews that represented the network and the show. I was given the kind of validation as an actor that people dream about. I got to go to awards shows, press junkets, roundtables, and fancy parties. I was driven and dressed and groomed. I grew up and became a professional actor during my time on this show. My life was defined by being on the show *24*. This included a new thing, called "being famous." People feel like they know you—that's how you know what you're doing is successful. What a weird way to live. And apparently it means not only that strangers feel like they know you but that they feel like they have the right to sometimes treat you like shit.

"Chloe!?" A man once yelled at me at the airport. I tried really hard to not hear him. Then he looked around to see if anyone else was seeing what he was seeing. Again, "Uh . . . Chloe!?" OK, so you're calling me by my character's name. I'm not Daniel Day Lewis—I don't walk around in character every day. I guess I need to remember that I'm in your house on your TV and you are invested in what my character is going through. This means I'm doing my job but it's not real life. You need to acclimate to me as a person. But you don't want to. You love my fictional world and it just came to life before your eyes like magic. You want me to scoop you up and take you on an adventure.

"Yeah, it's me, Chloe. I need a random person from the airport to help, someone like you, what's your name?"

"Vincent."

"OK, Vincent, you need to cancel your trip and come with me as an honorary counter-terrorist agent. Jack Bauer is incapacitated." He stares in wonderment.

"Vincent. Can you hear me? This is your mission if you choose to accept it. Take this firearm ..." I don't have that kind of time. Instead, I just sigh and put on a forced smile.

"Yeah, hi."

"You're Chloe! Where's Jack?"

"Yeah, I don't know, I guess he's still in that Russian prison ..."

"Chloe, why are you flying coach? I thought you were set for life."

I'm sorry, what? You can't ask someone that. It's part of the social code of being a person in a society. You don't go around asking other people how much money they make. How rude! But OK, you want to know if I made a lot of money. I get it. Huge show, lead part opposite Kiefer Sutherland. Multiple years. Sold to other countries and channels, won lots of Emmys and Golden Globes, changed the face of television.

The answer is yes. And no. I made a lot of money and, also, I spent that money! It wasn't that much money. People have an assumption about celebrity and wealth. Understandable. It makes sense that you would believe I was a millionaire when maybe at the height of my fortune I was a hundred thousandaire. It was a lot for me. I'm from Trenton, Michigan. We weren't taught how to have money or make money. We were taught to maybe get a job as a pipe fitter or at McDonald's. When I graduated high school, I was in no way ready for college. I didn't know what college prep was. The only reason I even knew what colleges were was from the flyers they would send in the mail addressed to current residents. "Current Resident"—that's me! I'm a "Current Resident." Junk mail was my guidance counselor.

I wasn't Kiefer Sutherland. I didn't grow up a movie star and the son of a movie star. I didn't know how to do it.

There was a bonus season to *24* after it was off the air. The network brought it back and it was set in England! How exciting. Also, I was finally a fixture on the show. The show needed my character. That's a little thing called leverage. But I forgot about the network's ability to make up the rules that go in its favor. I don't even think it ever was discussed beyond what the producers decided to tell me. But who knows. The producers told my lawyer, "We're shooting in England. So we don't have a lot of money." Oh OK. Of course. Got it. Do I get a point? (Which means I'll make more money after it airs.) No? OK, sounds good. I was given an amount of money that was the equivalent of some crumpets and jam to move my family. Then the people who owned the flat we found realized a TV star was moving in, so they decided to double the rent. The furniture was the cheapest and shittiest imaginable. Have you ever been on a couch so cheap that it pushes you off and yet it's also costing you more money than you're bringing in? It was made out of hard cardboard and should have had a sign that read "not for bodies." Anyway, despite the backaches, dry mouth (heating and cooling was a disaster), and damp, wrinkled clothes due to the invention of the tiny euro clothes washer that was also a dryer that fit in the space where an American would think the dishwasher is supposed to go, I was in London working, which is something I never knew was possible. I was being gouged to live in this subpar place that had a facade of being upscale.

It was still an amazing opportunity. We were there shooting for five months. I did spend a chunk of money to take my then husband and our son to Rome, Venice, and Florence during some last-minute downtime. It was a ridiculous amount of money because it was a last-minute booking, but I don't regret it for a second. It was a once-in-a-lifetime opportunity to see these places. But when we got back home, I already needed to find more work. Believe me, I wish I could have returned to the celebrity stereotype of settling into an estate and knitting while I redecorate during every moon cycle. Industrial? No. Farmhouse eclectic? That's so 2014. OK. Boho? Pillows. Just pillows everywhere. No tables, no chairs.

Even people in the business make assumptions. Six years later, I ran into a casting director at a coffee shop and she said, "Oh, I thought you lived in England now!"

"What?"

"Don't you live in England and film *24* there?" *No lady, I dragged my husband and child there for a few months and then it was over. My son took rugby and trampoline classes, and my husband rode the tube and went to pubs. Then we came home.*

"You fucking bitch. You are dead to me." I didn't say that. I laughed like it was such a cute gaffe.

"Oh! So the reason you haven't called me in to audition for the past six years was because you thought I was still doing the series there? That's so funny. Yeah, it was only five months. I've been trying to get work for the past five and a half years hahahaha."

I needed to work again. I could just call my mom and dad at Fox because I'm part of the Fox TV network family, right? I called them.

"It's me, your daughter. Any more jobs for me?"

Fox is like, "Who dis?" Dial tone . . .

That's not entirely true. I did one episode of *New Girl* for the minimum amount allowed by my union, and twenty years later I would do two episodes of *25 Words or Less*, the syndicated game show hosted by Meredith Vieira.

DON'T WORRY about me. I'm like a cockroach who is also a princess. I came back and I have a certain lifestyle. I go to the grocery store and get whatever I want. I don't even look at the price.

Fresh-squeezed orange juice? Don't mind if I do. Private Selection brand bacon? Put it in the basket. Twelve-pack of toilet paper? Don't need it, just want it.

Ten years after *24* was on the air I would walk into a bowling alley and see my face on the side of a *24*-themed pinball machine. My hair was blowing in the wind, my mouth was open, like they were trying to make pinball sexy? I was startled. Also, not the picture I would have chosen. Do I get a cut of that twenty-five or fifty cents every time a prepubescent boy puts it in that old-timey slot with his oily fingers and pumps his slippery hips up against that machine? Do I get a cut of that money? No, I don't. Just knowing that might be happening is all the payment I need. I'm in it for the art.

# WHEN I WORKED AT DENNY'S

Working at Denny's when you're sixteen is a big deal.

I had my share of challenging experiences, but none had prepared me to be a working woman. The time I thought I could put hair gel in perfectly for the first time and look like a member of A Flock of Seagulls? I could not. No, those were real new wave punk rockers—they knew what they were doing. And sure, I had used what little problem-solving skills I had to navigate starting my period on the day I was meant to go sailing. It's called a maxi-pad, you're welcome.

I filled out an application to work at Denny's in Downriver, Michigan. I was granted an interview with the manager. I didn't know what I was doing but I was going to do it anyway.

Dina was the upwardly mobile female manager on duty. Dina's hair had seen *Pretty Woman* too many times. My interview took place *inside* her eighties hair. She had really big bangs that just flowed over onto the other side of her part, which I got to slide down after the interview, out the front door and into my parents' gold Chevy Sprint. She wore a brocade vest. Oh, you're not sure what a brocade vest is? Do yourself a favor. Google "brocade vests" and skip the men's, go straight to the ladies'. I'll be here when you're done. And it's not a "lady's pirate vest"—don't insult me. It's a high-power, high-fashion, ultimate glamour power vest you'd be lucky to have in your closet. Like finding a hundred-dollar bill, this doesn't happen every day. This vest is burned in my memory—I wrote poems about it. The vest has its own journal in my personal library under my pillow. If I had to guess, I'd say she bought it at The Limited, but back when The Limited was limited. Exclusive. Widely available but they acted like it wasn't. Before The Limited gave up, it was for women who fucked on their own terms. The vest had a brocade design of both floral and paisley. Dull gold stitching. A rich fabric colored with bronze, green, and dusty rose. It had three buttons that were brushed with a somber brass color. And what was under the vest? Not her voluptuous breasts—get your minds out of the gutter. Over the breasts and under the vest? Probably a celery-hued collared blouse with capped sleeves.

Dina was so intimidating. Tough as nails. She asked questions like: "What's your name? Is the address on this application correct? So, you're in the tenth grade?"

"I don't know! This is hard! Let's just go our separate ways and wash our hands of this experience. We both have things we gotta do, lives to lead, bangs to grow out. I am picking up what you're putting down. I'm not good enough to be a busser! I get it!"

What I really said was: "Yeah . . . Uh-huh."

My disappearing mouse act was not going to cut it. I begged myself to say something.

"I'm in the tenth grade."

"Well, do you like the tenth grade?"

"Uh, no."

"Have you had any work experience, Mary?"

Denny's wasn't my first job but it might as well have been. I had only previously worked at the drugstore where my mom worked for going on twenty years. My older sisters both worked there and I worked their summer sidewalk sale, which was a hot step away from being a bona fide Hallmark girl. Being a Hallmark girl was akin to any kind of job that lets you exist mostly comatose and makes you wear a smock. My responsibilities included refilling the card displays. There had to be four cards, facing the correct direction with corresponding envelopes. Sometimes you'd be expected to open a new pack and replenish from empty. To see that card display on empty was harrowing. What kind of monster let this happen? Imagine perhaps a customer bought four of the same card! Unlikely story. Definitely a Hallmark girl slacking off on the previous shift. Oh wait, I was the only Hallmark girl.

I had many moments of shame working there, not about my lack of focus or shitty work ethic, but about how my life could be spent kneeling on a sea of gray industrial carpet, opening row after row of metal drawers to finger and file the most soulless messages ever printed by a lonely machine: "You make a difference." "Be who you've always been, proudly." Watered-down designs with glitter and cursive. One floral love message after the other, a "Sorry for Your Loss" next to "Best Grandpa in the World." The place where lost humans with no ability to express themselves go to spend four dollars to have Hallmark do it for them. The place where a husband goes to buy a thirty-dollar (in 1980s money) ornament that is supposed to say, "I'm sorry I grazed the butt of your coworker at the company party but I thought I was being supportive by canceling poker night and attending in the first place," but instead is just a sparkly butterfly and he hopes that will do the trick.

Even sadder are the people who go to Hallmark to "get something nice" like a Precious Moments figurine. (Precious Moments are these little ceramic Christian figurines. For example, one would be called something like "God's Fishing Hole." It would depict a dad fishing and an inspirational religious quote.) Some people would be really classy and buy the snowball collection. Or was it little babies with snowflakes? I couldn't possibly know because if I think about it any longer, I will be required by law to kill myself. I may be writing this for you but I will not give you my life. Anyway, those were more high end. So, yeah, I would have to go get the Precious Moments upon request, which required me to go to the back (that's an industry term for the back storage room of the store). That meant using my eyes to look at the number from the display model and matching that number to the box. To find the box was an odyssey requiring going through the boss's tunnel of funk. The tunnel was a slim dark corridor with her ashtrays, price guns, receipts, Diet Coke cans, and various dusty restock items that you had to pass through to find the storage room. Her name was Joyce. She had deeply hairsprayed front feathers, lots of gold chains, coral nails overgrown with the nail beds showing, yellow smokers' fingers, and a loud, fast, raspy voice. Someone was always cheating her. She was the life of the party. She was the only color in the place. You had to shimmy past her and turn the light on to the cockroach room where God's statue boxes were kept. No one cared to organize the boxes. There were five hundred nondescript cardboard boxes with numbers printed tiny on the corners. You had to get the right box; otherwise, the statues would be "uncollectible." It was hell to match those heavenly boxes to their owners.

Eventually, I did work the register there. It's funny because later in life I would have an extreme inability to work a cash register. Back then I somehow was able to do it. Maybe it was because it was a simpler cash register, like you would literally punch in the numbers. Later the numbers became long codes called SKUs. Way later I used to work at Seattle's Best Coffee and my brain couldn't grasp their register. I'm not sure if my brain couldn't grasp it, or if it was because I didn't care and wasn't interested. I would become bored staring at it. This would become a major theme in my life. I don't like memorizing. Which is ironic because my job centers around it. At the brain-deadening drugstore, I was pretty good at it, you know, getting the thing, ringing the thing, bagging the thing. It was really exciting to just complete the transaction.

And I was really proud of my counting-back-change ability, which is something that has gone by the wayside in the years since. People don't know how to do that. Or maybe I'm just really dumb. It's one of those things you don't think about. I had to be told how to do it and then it was very simple. Let's say someone gives you a twenty-dollar bill. And then it costs eleven dollars and change. You just count up from the number that it costs. Time and time again I've seen people not know how to do it. They would try to subtract from the total amount and all you have to do is simply count up from the price. I understand it's not the norm for people to pay with cash now because humans are becoming robots.

So that was really gratifying for me, my ability to count change. That was one of my finer moments. You get some pennies in there and you count up to some other change and some ones and some fives. Wow. You go ahead and give me a fifty-dollar bill. I'm not afraid. I'm going to set the big bill on the drawer so we both can see it, both parties. I'm gonna count you back up. Everybody's safe. The person's like, "Oh, that's the money I gave you," and I'm like, "Yeah, that's the money you gave me, bitch. I'm about to count you back up to that and give you your change." And then I'm going to go ahead and put the money in the till and guess what? Since it's a fifty-dollar bill it's going to go under the drawer. It's going to go under the drawer because that's where the big bills go. And when I run out of one-dollar bills, I'm going to pick up the thing and just block them up, get them all going the right way. Put that little cash register thing down there. It's exciting. I get a flutter of hope for the future when I see somebody changing a till. Yes! That's commerce in action! Yes! That's customer service happening right in front of me!

Why couldn't my tenth-grade mind tell Dina the Denny's manager that I had used the register at the drugstore and I knew how to count change?! These were valuable skills. I think I was too intimidated by her vest and hair. She must have factored that in because I got the job! I started as a busser. Remember, bussing is cleaning up other people's spittle and trash and the food that came out of their mouths. It was the eighties, a whole bacterial and viral lifetime ago. I watched as Tanya, H.B.I.C., "Head Bitch In Charge (of the morning weekend shift)," manhandled the entire nonsmoking section by herself. That was too big to be one person's station, too small to be the whole restaurant, but it might as well have been. If you got that whole back section, it was like a no-man's-land. No one bothered you. You'd be flying by two entire round booths and a bunch of deuces in between. You had your own coffee station. Who's going to come over there and stock your shit and refill your coffee? You are, while handling eight tables. You betcha. So I spent a lot of time being Tanya's busser and that's how I learned the ropes of Denny's. I watched her punching in those SKUs and thought, *Maybe one day that'll be me.*

Then it happened. "We're going to give you your own responsibility. We need you to make the ranch dressing." Oooh! Hold the phone. I'm going to need a couple of days to absorb this. Whoa! An industrial-size tub of everyone's favorite sauce that they put on everything? You're going to leave me with that responsibility? Leave me with the real buttermilk? With an extra large unheard-of-size envelope of Hidden Valley Ranch dressing powder, and also the largest whisk you've ever seen? The whisk that a giant would use? You're going to put me in the walk-in fridge with all those items and let me have at it? Trust me with that responsibility? Guess what, guys? I fucking nailed it. I whisked the shit out of that ranch dressing. I'm a ranch lover at heart. Who isn't? So I'm not going to disrespect the art of whisking a powder into a buttermilk. I'm not going to take a shit on that. I'm going to take my time. I'm going to be alert, use my eyes and my ears. I'm going to see if there is any of the powder stuck to the sides. Not on my watch. It's not going to go to the table unstirred.

Being responsible for the ranch dressing allows you certain privileges. You get to fucking be away from everybody. You're just metaphorically and literally chilling in the fridge, bent over one of those big tubs. I'm assuming that the people reading this are pretty hoity-toity and they don't know the ins and outs of a walk-in fridge, but you've seen it. You've probably gotten a look on Guy Fieri's show, or maybe you've seen the disaster that is a walk-in refrigerator with rats and spoiled food on *Bar Rescue*. I will say it was very neatly kept because Denny's is legit. I also found the frozen guacamole in a can quite refreshing for some reason. That's technology right there. Why have fresh when you can have frozen?

I didn't talk to anybody or hang out with anybody. All of my coworkers were older women. I was an outcast, but I didn't even think about it that way. I was just like, *This is reality. This is life.* There was the brocade-vest manager but she didn't have time for anyone. Then you had Kenny in the back in the grease. The waitresses were busy. I think they were nice? It was just me and the ranch dressing. But you know, I definitely had a vibe with the cook because we both understood grease on a deep level. He was a quiet guy with a chip on his shoulder and into heavy metal. You never knew if he was going to respond when you spoke to him. He had a permanent scowl and it was always an exciting day when he responded to "hi" with a disgruntled "hi" back. I would imagine having sex with him—he'd have to take off his greasy apron.

Eventually, I would get promoted to be a server. It turns out you have to actually memorize the SKUs. There was a SKU for every menu item. Next time you're in a Denny's or an IHOP or a Chili's, imagine every item in that book of a menu being a series of numbers that you need to know. If you didn't have the one you needed memorized, you'd have to take out a cheat sheet and take the extra twenty seconds to look that shit up. Not cool. There could be a line to use the register. I have since had many dreams about waiting tables where I'd go up to use the register and then I'd remember that no one fucking told me what my register code was. Then I'd remember that also no one told me what the table numbers were. And employees would be waiting on me to use the register and customers would be waiting on me for their orders and I'd be freaking out because it was all numbers and I didn't have the numbers. In every dream another server would do it all for me, so I still would never learn the codes.

It was stressful, but I learned and I executed. I didn't want to talk to anyone or look at anyone but I did it anyway. I got to the point where I could handle that whole back section by myself, including the coffee station. I could even do interactions with people! Oftentimes, the simplest exchange would be misconstrued due to a face I made. I didn't know what my face was doing. I couldn't just smile and focus on the order—I had other things running through my head, like: "Do these people even like each other?" or "Has this guy washed his hands in the past few weeks?" or simply "I don't know how to talk to you." Straightforward communication was lost on me. So, let's say a guy would order the chicken fried steak, but when he looked up to see if I had heard, my face would be all scrunched up. Then he would think there was something wrong with chicken fried steak as a choice, and I didn't know how to explain to him that it was just my face.

The time I got dined and ditched on was particularly traumatic. It was midnight. There was a five top of drunk belligerent assholes. We were in a fight simply because I chose to walk up to the table. That was enough for them to turn on me. If only I had the ability to match them in their drunken swagger. If only I could walk up to the table and act like I was in on the convo.

"Yeah, when Sheila grabbed that guy's crotch, I just about lost it! Hahaha. Right? Guys. Yeah, beers and stuff. How about a round of steaks for you bunch of dicks?" Instead, what happened was, they saw my timid scrunched up expression and immediately started making fun of my name.

"Are you ready to order?"

"I don't know, Maray Linn! What's good here, Marahhh Laneeee?," a woman with her shoes off, wearing a tiara, addressed me. I wish they would stop talking to me and looking at me. It was like they wanted to make fun of me and fuck me at the same time. And I was a hostage.

"Five chicken fried steaks and strawberry shakes. Got it." They got their food and forgot about terrorizing me. But the fun wasn't over. When I came back to pick up their plates, none of them were at the table. Were they all in the bathroom at the same time? That's weird. I went into the ladies' room, looking for the one scuzzy lady. She wasn't there. She must be getting the car. I waited. I stared at that men's bathroom door. Then I walked over to the front door and saw their Chevy Impala peel out of there. Holy shit. They left without paying their bill! My cheeks burned with humiliation. I felt like a moron. I had failed Denny's. I had lost them $37.59. My manager is going to kill me. I had to take the slow walk of shame to the manager on duty, Steve. He sighed and without looking at me pulled out his green elastic bracelet reserved for the special manager's key and made the adjustment to the bill. What a slow burn. This situation was way out of my realm. Maybe Dina wouldn't find out.

No such luck. Dina approached me on her next shift. She was giving me the side-eye and said, "How are you doing?"

"I'm fine," I murmured, head down.

"I heard about your dine and ditch."

"Yeah, I'm sorry about that."

"You should be. That's a profit loss for us."

"I know."

"If it happens again, you will have to pay the bill. I let it go this time. But don't let it happen again."

"I won't." She stared at me.

"Why don't I believe you?" Uh, because you're a bitch?

"Um, I don't know." She stared me down. "I promise, I won't let it happen again," I whimpered. Please let me off this dreaded hook.

"Do you know how?"

"How what?" I was exposed for being a dummy with zero life experience and zero ability to communicate.

"There shouldn't be enough time that you're away from the table when the bill is outstanding. You have to watch them like a hawk when the check is on the table." That's the last thing I wanted to do—even to someone I liked.

"Yeah, and I had station ten, which is right by the front door." She looked pissed.

"It doesn't matter where they were sitting! It's your job to make sure they don't go out that front door without paying. Got it?" The weird thing about it is, while I was being admonished and it felt bad, the bigger experience I was having was boredom and apathy. I really didn't care about the money Denny's was losing. The restaurant, the food, the money. I was embarrassed that happened to me but that was it. I wasn't really Denny's material and she was on to me.

I could make fun of her vest in my head all day long, but when it came time to balance the books on the sales for the night, that burden rested solely on Dina's shoulders. No wonder she's the boss! I wondered if I would ever be able to have the strength that Dina had. I would hate being a manager of a restaurant. There was just too much at stake and too many moving parts. I'd be better off being demoted to busgirl or, even better, dishwasher. It was a mistake letting me make the ranch.

Instead of beating up on myself and wishing for custodial work, I would have been better off realizing that I needed more life skills.

I wanted to be assertive, competent, and able to take accountability like Dina, Tanya, and Joyce. The only thing I could think to do was bleach my hair and get a nose piercing. The nose piercing only lasted one day. I did it myself in my parents' bathroom and then later when my dad saw it, he told me to take it out.

I needed that job at Denny's. It broke me out of the protective bubble of living at my parents'. Having that table walk without paying their bills forced me to deal with being accountable on the job. Besides losing the money, I also got to observe my authority over myself in the world. My defense mechanism was saying nothing and trying to be invisible. That didn't work for this job. I had to act, react, and be accountable. Most of the time, I didn't enjoy waiting tables at Denny's. I was never comfortable interacting with others, but there were times when I felt a sense of pride and slight exhilaration from being able to juggle tables and do it well. It was fun serving people—I just didn't like that talking and pleasantry part. It felt good to be able to be at this job with fully grown adults. I couldn't imagine staying there for years. But the two years I did spend there gave me the valuable experience to know what it means to be a working girl. This served me later for the many other jobs waiting tables I had before I became a professional actor.

# WATERCOLOR DREAMS
# AND ENGAGEMENT RINGS

The world at large seemed to me like something to be tolerated until I found something that gave me joy. I liked to paint. When my parents signed me up for a watercolor class in a strip mall with half a dozen sixty-year-old women, it was the highlight of my seventeen-year-old life. The class took place inside a framing store after hours. There were two long buffet-style tables set up and pushed together. We sat in a circle on folding chairs around the table.

The teacher, Helen, had a very specific aesthetic—I'd like to call it "Greeting Card Chic." You achieve it by copying designs from actual greeting cards! She told us to bring in our favorite watercolor floral or landscape from looking at greeting cards that featured watercolors. This was really doable and not intimidating. Also, picking out a card would be easy for me, as I was a Hallmark card aficionado! I could do this! I picked a "Congratulations on the birth of your baby!" card. It was a big brown teddy bear with blocks next to it. I was drawn to the animal world, and the design seemed easy enough to copy.

I sat there every week for two years with the gentle chitchat of senior citizens washing over me. Every week I looked forward to it. Sometimes I didn't physically feel like getting up and driving there, but I always wanted to go. Helen was the only one who cared if something wasn't going the way she wanted. It was exciting to watch her get worked up about a misshapen thorn on a rose, or if a wash of burnt sienna came out too dark she might yell out, "Shoot," then furiously apply a tiny puddle to the mistake and pat it out with the crumpled-up paper towel she kept in her left sleeve cuff. Then she'd aggressively dunk the misbehaving brush in to be rinsed rhythmically. I imagined her saying to the brush, "You! Picked! Up! Too! Much! Paint! And! Now! You! Will! Drown!" with every thrust. She waterboarded that brush but then it was over as quickly as it happened. One time she was so focused that she rinsed the brush in her coffee cup instead of the water! Helen! She talked to her paintings too, and they listened: "You go there." And "That's not enough."

We were so lucky whenever she called us over to watch her pull a big move, like sprinkling salt and seeing the paint repel around each granule. It was magic, reserved for just the right moment and just the right spot. Then some light yellow ochre for a fold in a flower. The flower was in the foreground; the part of the flower petal closest to us would always have the white of the paper left clean, so that part would pop forward, outlined by the brightest cleanest shade of warm red to make that rose petal jump off the page. I loved her excitement and how she always misplaced her glasses, and, for moments at a time, I was convinced she would forget where she was.

She'd make laps around the table to stand over your shoulder and give expert suggestions: "I'd like to see the bear's ear pop a little more. Also, I can't tell what the bear is thinking. Do you know? See if you can depict that in your painting..." That's some deep shit.

I hated actual school. Aside from the extracurricular watercolor class and theater class, I didn't know how I would apply it to my benefit. So I leaned into "flying under the radar" and got by, got along, while biding my time. When I got to the end of high school, two of my best friends were getting into esteemed colleges. I could go to college and repeat all these classes I took in high school and be around other college students. Gross. The idea of a keg party and having to care about my college's sports teams was mind-numbing.

Maybe I could follow in my sister's or my mother's footsteps. My sister worked at a credit union and that was a big deal because she was paid twelve dollars an hour! My mom moved up the ladder at the drugstore going from cashier to pharmacist's technician. She took a test or a course and was making fourteen dollars an hour!

My guidance counselor was junk mail, so when I got a flyer for the Art Institute of Chicago, I took it as a sign. In the photo was the front of the art institute, a beautiful old building with grand steps up to the massive doors, and that was all I needed to know about the school. My imagination created the rest. I saw myself in a beret with an old-fashioned palette, deep in concentration, wearing a smock with paint splatters, holding a brush in my mouth. Then maybe I'd walk down some city streets or sit in an old lecture hall like in *Dead Poets Society*. I could be a highly regarded intellectual who hangs out at museums.

Then I looked at the price of the college and that idea went right out the window, so I looked for an art school nearby. There was one called the Center for Creative Studies in Detroit. It was also way too much money but I wanted to go more than anything. The center had a recruitment day where you'd bring your portfolio to show the teachers. I didn't have a portfolio. I had only whatever was assigned in high school and the watercolors from Helen's class. I imagined those wouldn't be good enough. I needed more.

My high school teacher had exposed me to different materials so that I wasn't afraid of them. I went and got myself a pad of paper and did some lame-ass portrait. It was a self-portrait. Then I set up some soup cans and an apple and drew that. I also put in a painting of some roses I had done in watercolor for my sister's anniversary. I really pulled the wool over the eyes of the faculty on recruitment day. They told me I was good! I felt so proud, and like there was a chance I belonged somewhere.

I began the process of applying to art school and was not only accepted, but also I was awarded a partial scholarship. I took out a student loan and borrowed my parents' car to commute to school. The first day I drove onto the parking lot, I felt like I belonged. Like one of the kids from the movie *Fame*, but I didn't dance and I didn't want fame. I just wanted to be an artist. I knew that a part of me that was buried was beginning to sing. Being in touch with the idea of being an artist thrilled me.

It turns out there was a whole wing of the school for people studying car design and product design. Yuck. Why would you make something useful when you could make something solely to express yourself? The product and car design was what funded the whole school. Those students got legitimate high-paying jobs and were very skilled. Fine art has never made anyone money, but we believed we were the only thing important in the school.

There was one teacher, Mr. Pennington, who took us on a walk-about to the Art Institute of Detroit. He was flamboyant and wore a tweed jacket with a vest and a bow tie, and his hair was parted on the side. He was pretentious, but I needed that in my life. He made the dream real, something tangible that I could sink my teeth into. He pointed to a stapler and then a Rodin sculpture and said, "See? Artists! Artists designed everything, whether it's fine art or an everyday object, somebody has to design it. An artist designs the world." And then he'd say, "What is art? Do you have what it takes to live the artist's lifestyle?" I listened to him talk and take us around and show us things in the world and discuss their lines and their inherent beauty. I listened to him with wonder. My face belied emotion but inside I was smiling and I thought, *I think I've got what it takes*.

There was a guy in my sculpture class, his name was Wayne. He had a big smile and a big laugh. But the smile was too big and the laugh was too loud. He asked me out. I didn't really want to go out with him, but I didn't know how to say no. He was fun to talk to. I would have liked to be "just friends" with him. I did not have the capacity to say that because I always lived by the rule that if someone shows interest in you, you have to go along with it. (I'm still trying to change this behavior.) He wanted me, adored me, and I was flattered. So eight months later, Wayne asked me to marry him. I said yes because, again, he was really putting himself out there. We went to Kay Jewelers in the mall and picked out a lovely solitaire diamond for me. I was afraid to put it on, so I put it on a ribbon around my neck so I could hide it under my shirt. Yes, that was the inspiration for the *Sex and the City* episode (that's what I tell myself).

I would showboat it around when we were with each other and I knew I wouldn't run into anyone I knew. I was embarrassed. It seemed silly to be engaged.

I remember Wayne inviting me over to his parents' house. The dinner was super awkward. My family didn't talk at dinner either, but to sit with someone else's uptight family who didn't talk was excruciating. At least with my own family, it was our own not talking. I was the guest of honor too, so there was pressure for me to yak it up and really be the princess I was supposed to be. His whole family knew he had asked me to marry him. How embarrassing. The dinner was something pedestrian like breaded pork chops and green beans from a can. Everyone was given a full glass of milk. His mom was super excited and really sweet, which was supposed to make me feel really good but did not. "Welcome to the family!" She gushed. The dad and the older brother nodded in agreement. I suddenly felt objectified by his mom—all of her daughter-in-law dreams instantly got placed on my shoulders. I could almost see her looking for my baby bump. It was awful.

I avoided telling my mother, but each day our engagement got more real so I knew I had to bite the bullet. "I need to talk to you." She met me at the door, worried: Sensing the badness of what I was about to say, she pushed us to the front porch to talk.

"What is it?"

I was delirious, a young woman trying to project that I was doing something important and responsible. When really it was the desperate strung-out energy of being in reaction to the world and not driven by my own convictions or sense of self. I pulled out the ring and showed it to her in the palm of my hand.

"I'm engaged to Wayne!" I smiled way bigger than was natural to make it like a movie moment. She was enraged.

"Don't tell your father," she hissed. So I didn't and I never said another word to her about it. In that moment I was too small, ashamed that my idea didn't fit with my mother's idea of what I should be doing. I felt guilty and I was angry. This was not how I wanted her to react. Suddenly I wanted to leave. I wanted to run away somewhere else where I didn't have to deal with my fiancé, his mother, or my mother. I didn't want any of this.

Soon, even my desire to prove my mother wrong was not enough to keep the relationship with Wayne going. The engagement made it glaringly obvious to me that Wayne was not to be my husband simply because he asked. In my heart I knew that he was not a guy I wanted to be attached to for years. I held out through that Thanksgiving, then Christmas, and then it was the end of the school year. I had to break up with Wayne. I couldn't go through another summer as his fiancé. We were set to go out for pizza and right after we settled into our garlic rolls appetizer, I laid it on him. "I can't get married," I told him with tears in my eyes. "I think there's something bigger for me out there." He was stunned.

"What about our marriage?"

"I can't do it." I was so upset to hurt him but exhilarated by the wide-open life that lay before me. I could go anywhere and be anything I wanted.

There was an end-of-the-year show. We all got to display a couple of pieces from our last series of work for the semester. Mine were a couple Basquiat-like paintings. My friend Tara showed some small sculptural nests that contained her dog's nail clippings. (That was when I decided to get some distance from my friendship with Tara.) Anyway, the parents were invited to come see all of the student work. We were all mingling outside in between the concrete pillars at the reception when I saw Wayne's mother. She gave me the look of death. I relished all four seconds of it. *Yes, I am the woman who broke your son's heart. Get a good look, lady, because this is the last time you're going to lay eyes on this hot piece of ass.* I didn't know where I was going, but I knew I wasn't going to stay there.

# IF THIS IS WHAT COMEDY IS, IT'S NOT FOR ME

The first summer after my first year at art school, my best friend from high school said I could stay with her in Ann Arbor, Michigan, on the U of M campus in her apartment with her and her roommate. She may not have been serious and it might not have been a good idea, but I took her up on it anyway. I got a miserable job at Olive Garden and I believe I slept on the floor between her and her roommate. I blocked it out.

During my awake hours, I felt like I was under water in my life. I decided to take action by joining an improv class in a fake chalet restaurant banquet room led by a U of M student. I hadn't seen improv before. I did not understand what the improv teacher student was saying. I did not speak in class. One day he gave us sheets of paper and told us to make two columns, one with an activity we enjoyed. I wrote "eating breakfast" and then wrote down all the aspects of eating breakfast: picking up the fork, pancakes with butter and syrup, napkin. In the other column you'd pick something that is the opposite of breakfast, like trying to escape your car after it swerved into the Hudson River and is sinking: panic, imminent death, pressure, drowning. Then you'd pick one item from each column and put them together in a scenario and that's how you'd write jokes. So it would be "syrupy imminent death" or "pancake pressure."

I didn't think any of it was funny. I blamed myself for not understanding the assignment, but I was also angry that it was so dumb. I didn't understand why that would be funny or why that would even mean anything. I hated the class and the teacher. *If this is what comedy is, it's not for me.* At the time I thought I didn't measure up, didn't know how to do improv the correct way. It didn't make sense and was profoundly boring. Somehow I stayed in the class long enough to put on the show at the end. I did a sketch with two other people where I was literally clucking like a chicken while some guy improvised that he was selling me to a girl with long dark hair. There was nothing even remotely funny about it.

In the parking lot after, I met this guy named Steve Charles, who had been at the show. He wasn't in the class because, as he would eventually let me know, he was an improv master. That night, he was directing traffic as part of a real-life comedic improv he was performing, like Andy Kaufman but with no audience. He wore a whistle around his neck, black pleated pants, and a red T-shirt tucked in like an eighties maitre d'. I was enamored with his command of himself in the world. His behavior was embarrassing but I was attracted. He told me, "Comedy is my life," and I believed him. I had no clue that comedy would actually become *my* life.

He would do bits with the cashier at Dunkin' Donuts. Aggressive bits that the other person was subjected to. It was awful. We ended up falling madly in love. I think what got me is that he told me, "I don't usually date girls like you," and then showed me pictures of models that he usually dates. I complimented him on his choice and ability to get hot women.

Eventually, he became obsessed with me because I created the space to listen to all of his journal entries; I accepted who he said he was. He demanded my attention and was jealous if I talked to other men.

One night Steve Charles was very excited to do stand-up comedy at an open mic in a sports bar called Cherry's in Canton, Michigan. Of course, I was there in the audience supporting him. One of his best jokes was about when he's at a bar he likes to pretend he is the host and offer people the drink condiments as snacks. "Would you like a lemon, lime, or cherries?" I sat on a barstool cheering for him but I also kept hearing a louder voice in my head saying, "I could do this!"

The next week, I got up on that stage. It's a mystery to me why I was compelled to do it, but I had pieces of paper taped to my legs and arms and was reading off of them. While people watched the Lions game, I tried to distract them with my performance, which was reading a list of nonsensical words and bits of advertisements and phrases from common sayings, all coming out of my mouth with pauses in between for the audience to react. "Waxy buildup? We've got you covered!" Pause. "Tragic circumstances led to her untimely death." Pause. "You're hired." "I'd love to see your new project. Meet me at the lagoon, tomorrow around two?" This was some capital, high-concept stuff. People didn't know what to make of me. Anything could happen. They weren't sure if I was OK. They laughed at the awkward space in between my phrases. I thought it was a huge success. There was no semblance of joke writing on my part, which would become a theme of my performances. I guess I thought I was the joke. The fact that I was standing on stage trying to say something, anything, was funny to me.

Steve Charles convinced me I should quit school to go camping in Lithuania with him. I thought this guy was a jackass, but at the time I took his overbearing childish behavior to mean we were passionately in love. To me he was selfish and cruel. I watched him take his grandmother's credit card to buy things for himself without her knowing, and I still stayed with him after that. I guess I was so desperate for attention that I allowed myself to look the other way.

When I finally did break up with Steve, a fellow server at a restaurant I worked at let me stay at her place. It seemed like every day he was at her door looking for me. I hid in her room, and she would pretend I wasn't there. The guy who made a habit of saying I wasn't good enough for him was now obsessed with me. I think he couldn't accept being broken up with. Now that I was in my friend's space, it was clear how ridiculous his behavior was.

He begged me for another chance. I was embarrassed but not strong enough to really break it off with him. I was way out of love but now was scared of what he might do. We hung out a few more times until I could escape back to my parents' house. My shame-filled relationship came to a close. He and I never spoke again.

# RUSH LIMBAUGH

In June 2006 I was invited to go to Washington, DC, and partici-
pate in a forum about *24*. The show had a strong conservative audience that consisted of not only regular TV viewers but also people
in Washington. They liked the show's nationalistic themes and the
accurate depictions of the complexity and seriousness of homeland
security work. The show itself premiered less than a month after
9/11. The event was sponsored by a right-wing policy think tank,
and it was really just an excuse for them to get people from the
show they loved to the Capitol. They flew a few of us actors and
producers up to Washington, DC, and showed us around. They
had a big dinner for us. At dinner I was seated next to Secretary of
Homeland Security Michael Chertoff. As someone who had previously gone to therapy for social anxiety, I still did not have the
ability to make small talk. (Here's a hot tip: If you go to therapy, be
prepared to talk about yourself! Don't sit across from the therapist
asking her, "How are you today? What did you do after lunch?" I
spent three thousand dollars one year to help the therapist plan her

son's bar mitzvah.) I didn't know how to talk to people that I had stuff in common with let alone high-ranking government officials. I had no idea where to begin with this guy. I spouted some comedy, some non sequiturs to break up all of the dry conversation and false humility going on around the place.

The day of the event I put on my seersucker A-line skirt that I bought for this occasion at Ross Dress for Less and made my way to the Ronald Reagan International Trade Center amphitheater.

The topic of the forum was "*24* and America's Image in Fighting Terrorism: Fact or Fiction, Does It Matter?" It was a discussion about whether the fictional techniques used on the TV show influenced the tactics of government and the military in real life. The panel featured myself as well as the co-creators of *24*, Joel Surnow and Robert Cochran, producer Howard Gordon, and a couple of people who studied or worked with homeland security policy. Michael Chertoff gave the opening remarks. Rush Limbaugh moderated the panel. I don't remember much of what was talked about or what I contributed, but in researching this event from my past I found an ABC News article written by America's own Jake Tapper, who beautifully captured my experience. He wrote that I exclaimed that I didn't know what I was doing there, what was going on, or who I am anymore. Rajskub said being embraced by the power structure in Washington is "sort of odd, you know? I don't really know what to think of it. I really am kind of beside myself and speechless to be here, it's really very, very strange." He also remarked that I gave Justice Thomas a shout-out asking him what to say. Apparently I said I need to start reading more if I'm going to be invited to Washington.

Thank you, Jake Tapper, for your accurate reporting. This is why we need journalists. What I do recall is at the beginning of the panel Rush Limbaugh walked behind us and introduced everyone. When he got to me, his way of saying "hello" was to bend down behind me. I turned to look up and that's when it happened. When I turned he was coming down to give me a kiss . . . on the lips?! I have no idea how he got his body around so quickly for a full-on kiss. As it happened, tons of camera flashes went out. He had to have known what he was doing. He knew there were ten photographers there—I did not. I should have but I didn't. I also didn't know how to stop the kiss from happening.

In one shrewd move of his, an image went out into the world that showed I was a supporter of the right-wing cause. I was not. It also showed I found Rush Limbaugh attractive. I did not. The kiss was weird. Intentional for him, and accidental for me.

It was a big moment in the news cycle. I remember getting calls during the days following. Even NPR called me to get a statement on it. An ex-boyfriend of mine who had a lot of musician friends called me in a state of fury,

"How could you be dating Rush Limbaugh?" I told him I wasn't numerous times because he kept repeating it until he followed up with telling me the members of my favorite indie rock band were no longer fans of mine. He read that.

I went along with a lot of publicity stuff for work. I knew I was shilling for the success of the show, to keep my job, to stay on the air, and to take the spotlight when the show was in the spotlight. But to become a right-wing darling was too much. Thank god it didn't last more than one news cycle. I still don't understand what Michael Chertoff did as Homeland Security secretary.

# FROM ONE ART SCHOOL TO ANOTHER

I had a friend in art school who lived north of Detroit. I lived south of Detroit. Instead of commuting from her parents like I did, she had an apartment on campus in the penthouse suite of the old art deco building. I guess her dad wanted her to be comfortable and not have to drive back and forth to school. She loved Nirvana and Alanis Morisette. She related to artists who were misunderstood like her. One time she had me over for lunch. She made her famous open-faced tuna melts on Thomas' English Muffins with Kraft cheese slices in her toaster oven. They were delicious but I couldn't help but be haunted by the discarded tuna can in the sink. There were flies and gnats and *why couldn't she just rinse the can real quick?*

The third year of art school in Detroit was for studio art. It was when you got to advance to the next level and get your own studio to begin your body of work as a serious artist. I was still in my second year, so I had this to look forward to. The problem, however, was that the studios were more like closets. They had no windows and no shelving. Just some lights, an easel, and cement walls. You couldn't even back up to look at your painting. The best part was the hallway, where you could get out of your messy hot box and see people. A few of my friends were a year ahead and already getting their studios. This girl named Trina had a studio—her paintings were brutally boring. I couldn't imagine being a neighbor to her studio and having to take her brown on brown rain paintings seriously.

It was now the beginning of our third year and my tuna-fish-can friend Kelly told me she was going to take her studio year in San Francisco. What the F? No one told me about this! I didn't even know that was an option. Our school has a sister school? I needed to go too. Sure, there was my rational brain yapping on about how, "You can't just do that because she is, you can't pick up and go! How will you afford it? You've never been to California. You don't know anything about it. It's probably too hard to get in . . ." But I knew I would do whatever it took to make it happen. It was a feeling that propelled me forward—no wasn't an option.

I told Kelly I wanted to go. She was excited and said we could be roommates! I was too late for the application process, but I convinced my school and the school in San Francisco that I needed to go with my friend. They ended up letting me in. Sometimes when you ask for what you want, it's not that hard to get. I told my parents and blew their minds.

When it was time for us to drive to San Francisco from the suburbs of Detroit, Kelly came to pick me up in the brand-new Toyota Corolla her dad had bought her. I was standing on my parents' porch with two black Hefty trash bags full of my clothes and things I was going to take with me. She pulled into the driveway and I looked in her car. It was completely full with her stuff. There was a small space in the front seat for me, surrounded by bags in the back and in the center of the car. There was a large rain stick. Yeah, I said rain stick. I think this was part of her spiritual practice and she had it in the center of the car. When I saw this, I dropped one of my trash bags. I left it on the driveway and got in the car and we drove across the country.

Kelly and her dad had gotten us an apartment. I was so lucky! Our apartment was in Noe Valley. It was $375 per person a month. It had a little kitchen and living room with each of our bedrooms on either side. We started our new life, and as the days went on, I was more and more in my head. Kelly had set up her whole altar to nourish her spirit. It had her collections of beads, incense, crystals, stones, scarves. She would add to it as objects spoke to her. I was spiritual too. My sacred space was a futon on the floor, no pillow, no sheets, with my few bits of clothing on the floor next to me. That's how I got in touch with the universe. Her messages from the universe were about love, oneness, and sensuality. Mine were like, "You need to get a job. Yesterday!"

The waiting-tables job market was saturated. I was real hot shit in Detroit, I was Olive Garden trained. I knew how to pair breadsticks with a Kendall-Jackson cabernet. They would be lucky to have me here in SF. I walked up and down the streets in Haight-Ashbury, the Mission, going into every restaurant, one after the other, asking if I could fill out an application. I can't imagine what I looked like. I wonder if I showered. I wasn't even close to being handed an application.

While Kelly was getting in touch with her vibes through smoking pot and meditation, I would cry and pray to somehow be able to stay in San Francisco. I loved taking the streetcar through Chinatown to campus. I loved everything about the city. All the students in school were pretentious and it was outrageously expensive, but going back to Michigan was not an option. Kelly would tell me that it was going to be OK. I wanted to scream at her, "You don't get it!" Instead, I let her take me out to lunch and then shave the back of my head.

I ended up getting a minimum-wage job at Double Rainbow Ice Cream for $3.75 an hour. I would have one burrito a day, and on those days that I worked shifts at Double Rainbow Ice Cream, I would craft elaborate ice cream meals. You would start with, you know, maybe vanilla as an appetizer. Then, an ice cream flavor that's got some girth to it, such as a chocolate peanut butter. That's going to be your heaviest entrée of ice cream—you know, more like a chicken parmesan. Then back to a lighter dish like cookie dough ice cream. You would be sure to cleanse your palate in between each course with a lemon or raspberry sorbet. Every once in a while I would make myself a milkshake. That would be a special day. I'd just eat ice cream the entire shift and really ride that line of being sick.

One night at Double Rainbow Ice Cream I realized I had a project due for my performance art class the very next day. Since it was eight o'clock at night, I made a decision to steal a five-gallon tub of ice cream. Somehow I fit it into the freezer at the apartment? This part of the story is hazy. Maybe I stole it and went straight to school. I'm a criminal. I took it to class in the morning and made the piece about the ice cream, carrying it on the bus and the passage of time.

If you don't know what performance art is, let me tell you: It's when the art world went off the rails. When Pop art became conceptual art and then conceptual art could not be contained with materials. The artist and their actions became part of the art. Sound, time, space, and smell could all factor in. You could say it started in with the Surrealists and the Fluxus movement, who staged performances to challenge the elitism of the art world. The performance artists of the early 1970s were an extension of that. Yoko Ono and John Lennon did performance art pieces that broke the rules of traditional art but also had a focus on feminism, activism, and blurring the line between art and life. There were a lot of performance artists from my school. A famous one came back to speak to our class. Her name was Lydia Lunch and one of her pieces was vomiting in a trash can. Karen Finley was perhaps channeling the devil when she howled and spoke while nude but covered in chocolate, pulling a scroll from her vagina. I think it was a piece about her dad. A lot of the famous pieces had shock value, some were more ethereal, videos on an endless loop.

It was a perfect medium for me. I was attracted to being a performer, but I didn't know what I wanted to say or who I was yet. I could explore and feel safe.

The other students had no problem taking themselves seriously. There was the guy who taped his genitals to the side and put on lipstick in a mirror without saying a word. He sat on the floor, acting like we weren't there. The whole class sat on the floor watching him until he was done with whatever he decided to do. That's the thing about performance art: There usually is no beginning or end. Maybe some crescendos, but since the narrative idea of beginning, middle, and end doesn't have to be adhered to, anything goes! These types of pieces ride on the ego and salesmanship of the artist. That piece was about self and identity.

An obese woman set up a ton of butter pats in a row like dominoes. Her piece began when she got on the floor and slowly crawled to pick each one up. I felt her personal pain of eating too much butter. Another piece was a guy and a girl who got into human-size black socks. They looked like worms. The piece was watching them try to get down a flight of stairs without breaking their necks. For another guy's piece, he took us to the second story of the school, went on a ledge, and jumped from the ledge to a tree that was in the yard. The purpose? For us to see if he made it or not. He did make it, barely. He slammed into the tree. That wasn't even my favorite piece.

My favorite bad performance art piece was a guy who showed us that he was baking bread in two breadmakers. Then we left the classroom and we waited about forty-five minutes until the bread was done. We came back in and he fed us warm homemade bread, which, by the way, was delicious. Then he informed us that half the bread had plaster from the wall in it and half of it didn't. The piece was about communism.

My performances eventually became more than melted ice cream. Unlike the butter pats and human worms, my pieces were story oriented. More like theater. For one of my pieces I played a character who was half pirate, half Peter Pan. I had built a circular cardboard structure and I did a gibberish monologue from inside of it about collecting the heads of pirates. No one could see me. I threw heads I had made yelling, "Off with her head! I've got the pirate in hand, matey! He's dead!" With each exclamation a head got thrown over. If you sat down with a piece of paper and wrote out random words then made those random words exist in the physical world—that was my piece.

For one of my more dramatic performances, my foot was tied to the ceiling and there was a stool with a bowl of jelly beans just out of my reach; a makeshift spotlight shined on me to maximum effect. I launched into a monologue about how my husband tied me up to the ceiling and left! For this one, I remember actually writing out a monologue instead of improvising. My husband had no regard for my feelings and our marriage was crumbling. I was sick of being the doting wife who did what he told me. It was profound. Especially since I didn't have a husband and no one was making me do anything.

For one of my other pieces, there was a podium made out of cardboard. I dressed up in an oversized man's suit that I got from a thrift store. Using a conductor's wand made out of a wire hanger, I tried to give a speech. My papers were all mixed up and dropping to the ground, and the podium kept collapsing. Again, with the random words, I was playing a character who was flustered and supposed to present and couldn't get the words out. This piece was the closest to who I was, underdeveloped and unable to express myself. I didn't know what I wanted to say nor did I have the tools to say it. People laughed at my attempts. It was the closest to my vision for my art and the truest form of my expression, and it felt incredible to be able to perform in front of people. It had not occurred to me that what I was doing was comedy.

I started going to open mics in the Mission District a few times a week. Performing was the only thing I cared about. Of course, there were relationships. There was always a relationship. But my favorite thing and my main focus was going to rooms where I could perform. Bars and cafés had shows where you could say whatever you wanted into a microphone in front of the patrons. Like poetry. I did it. Again, you guessed it, I read aloud random words I put together in my journal.

Comedians also would come to the open mics. It was a time when comedy clubs were starting to close and alternative rooms were opening. One night, I saw Patton Oswalt. I didn't know he was a stand-up comedian. His performance was confident, eloquent, and seemed casual and off-the-cuff. He seemed to have a sense of morality, and I believed that he was telling his own personal truth while not taking himself seriously. I wanted that. He knew exactly how to tell a story. It was polished and you didn't worry for him. Patton's performance was personal but it was entertaining first and he was in complete control of how he sounded and what he looked like.

There was an older hippie guy named Daniel who used to frequent the same open mic as me at the Bottom of the Hill club. He was from Humboldt County (north of San Francisco . . . drive until you hit the remote woods). He was a nice enough guy. Now that I really know about guys and myself, yes he wanted to fuck me. At the time, I just thought he wanted to talk to me. I remember him telling me about his Airstream trailer and how he grew pot. This was back before people talked about growing pot. He was enamored with me. Daniel was not attractive. He thought he was. I didn't want him to feel bad, so I let him flirt with me.

One night my friends were on stage singing their deconstructed version of David Bowie's "Life on Mars?" and I was standing next to Daniel. He asked me why I was mocking poetry in my last few performances. Didn't he get it? I can't be earnest and try to recite poetry. That's so gross now that I knew about comedy. *You have to evolve, Daniel.* He looked at me with his crinkly eyes, overgrown gray beard, hand-rolled cig in the air between his fingers and said, "Why comedy?" He was disappointed in me like a dad. His mouth was pursed to show his pity toward me, and he shook his head slightly as if to say: "How could you ruin the holy grail of poetry?" Because it was never holy to me. *Your seriousness is ruining your personality*, I wanted to tell him. *I will definitely not be going to your Airstream in the woods now. The very disappointment you expressed toward me for making fun of poetry is equal to the disdain I now have toward you.* I can see now that everything is comedy, especially poetry.

At an open mic in the back of a bar called The 500 Club in San Francisco, I met an older man named Ramon. Ramon wore jumpsuits and eyeshadow, and was prone to interject jokes about the Holocaust or break into a refrain of "Close to You" by the Carpenters at any moment. He was a wizened comic who was on the scene before us youngsters showed up. He was respectful and kind, but also acerbic and observant. He made a point of not giving a crap. He practiced standing out in public places. He was an elevated, professional Steve Charles.

He would sing loudly on the bus and look forward as if he didn't notice others looking at him. At heart, he was a hippie from Santa Barbara. Word on the street was that Robin Williams stole aspects of his persona and that's what made him famous, while Ramon haunted all the old clubs and coffee shops locally, remaining unknown. It was also rumored that he used to do cocaine, went to jail for it, and that's why he was sober. Well, sober but still smoked weed all day, drank coffee, and smoked cigarettes.

He took me to the butch lesbian breakfast place, the jazz club, museums. When I made a little bit of money, he took me to the bank and made me open a bank account. I didn't know how to do this or that I could. It was a Bank of America. He was a real friend.

One time we lay on my couch together; it was narrow and there wasn't room for both of us. His lips brushed against mine almost by the sheer weight of energy he was holding in. Almost involuntarily. And then it was over. We lay next to each other, his body anxious and coursing with unexpressed sexual energy. I think he really needed to have sex but he wouldn't let himself. I loved him but wasn't attracted to him. I wanted to be around him and not him as a friend. At a certain point of us hanging out, I thought, *I'll probably just do it with him, for him, because I know he needs to.* He needs to use this energy and it wouldn't be so bad. So I reached out to him ever so slightly, but he never turned over and I was too terrified to do anything else. He told me he was moving from San Francisco back to LA.

A few months later, I got invited to go to LA shows with the comedians I had met in San Fran. I didn't have a car. I had two hundred dollars. I don't really remember bringing anything. Ramon said I could stay with him, so I hitched a ride with Blaine Capatch, a fellow comedian friend.

# HOW TO FIND YOUR LIFE'S PURPOSE IN THREE HUNDRED INDECIPHERABLE, NOT-EASY STEPS

Ramon's place was in a suburb of LA called Sherman Oaks. He lived rent free in a house that was owned by his manager. I didn't know he had a manager and didn't know what a manager was, but I found out it was a big deal. The manager had high-profile clients like Drew Carey, Tim Allen, and Janeane Garofalo. (Eventually, I would be represented by a junior manager named Dave Rath, but I had no idea at the time that this was my future.) There were two other guys who lived at the house, unknown behind-the-scenes comedy writers and stand-ups from New York. Their names were Jeff and Mark. They seemed to be in their forties. Suddenly, I was in proximity to people who were in proximity to huge success! It was very exciting. I slept on a futon in the foyer. That didn't go very well, so I started to sleep in Ramon's bed with him. The house reminded me of the *Brady Bunch* house if it had fallen into disrepair and been taken over by three adult men.

Across from Ramon's bedroom was the bathroom, where the toilet would overflow and the water would soak into the carpet.

The carpet was floating. You had to walk on soggy carpet to use the bathroom. It was very alarming, but what could I do? I had zero dollars and didn't know where I was—I was invisible.

They were always pot smoking, which I didn't really know that much about. I hadn't been around it as far as it being a household item. That was the first time I saw a bong as a permanent fixture on the coffee table because weed smoking was the daily breakfast. The other staples were Cheez-Its, vodka, and watermelon. These seemed to be the only food items. I personally don't remember eating during this time. There was also a lizard that stayed in the backyard by the pool. He was humongous, like two and a half feet long. Staying here was scary and refreshing.

One day, Blaine Capatch (the comedian friend who had driven me to LA) picked me up in a little red hatchback to go to a show.

We drove on this magical street called Laurel Canyon. The street goes through a canyon that goes from the San Fernando Valley and empties into a place called West Hollywood. I had never been on a road that was through a canyon; it twisted and turned until we came out the other end. We magically landed at the bottom, which was Sunset Boulevard. There was a Wolfgang Puck's in a strip mall and a movie theater and a Buzz Coffee. It was pre-Starbucks time. We made a right turn and I saw Book Soup and Tower Records and I almost started crying. It felt like the most beautiful thing I had ever seen. That's when I knew: West Hollywood was my new boyfriend.

The show was at a place called the Spades Club. The Spades Club, we heard, was partly owned by Slim Jim, a former member of the eighties band the Stray Cats. When I was in middle school, I had a baseball T-shirt with the logo of the Stray Cats and I had a curly perm. I would put hair gel on the top of my hair to have a single curl on my forehead to look like the Stray Cats. This was a fact I have shared with nobody. There's a handful of people that would remember those fateful days in the seventh grade where I made this fangirl gender-swapping fashion choice. It's up to you what you do with that information.

This secret club, Slim Jim's side project, was in Hollywood. I guess he just wanted a cool club. You would think he would have bands playing there. It turns out, they didn't get that far in the planning. The club was in the bottom of a bank building; you had to find the door, get to the basement, go through some abandoned office spaces to get there. There, in the bowels of the basement of this building, were cheap floor lights and curtains. A couple of cheap walls were erected to create a doorway. There were bargain chairs and tables, and a bar was built out of materials that looked as if a Marriott Hotel had gifted their old bar in chunks to be reassembled in a configuration in the hopes that it would function. Two or three girls were employed to wait on the customers and the bar did take American dollars. There was a stage and a sound system. I was expecting more glamour, something more established. This place felt like we weren't supposed to be there—it wasn't supposed to be a club—and that we were going to be kicked out or it was going to be shut down any minute. Every time I went there, I wondered if Brian Setzer would show up. Probably not, he's busy with his big band; also, the Stray Cats probably aren't even friends anymore. But Slim Jim would have to show up, right? I mean, it's his club. He would want to check out business, enjoy the show. Play in his new band at the club. I don't even know if I would recognize him. I was too afraid to ask my new potential group of friends if they had ever seen him. I didn't want to be lame and I figured someone would mention it, if he was ever there.

The show was created and hosted by Laura Milligan; she was in character as a former child actor, Tawny Port, who wrote poetry, hosted a show, and put her friends on stage. She was re-creating in fiction and comedy all the pretentious open mics I had been to in San Francisco. An anything-goes variety show, the weirder the better. Characters blurred the line between being in character and being a person off the street. David Cross used to do a character who was self-righteous and ranting about the government. The monologue would build until he was going to make a monumental personal act of rebellion and purpose by taking a shit on the American flag. If I'm remembering correctly, the piece ended with his character not being able to execute the bowel movement and leaving the stage in shame.

Jack Black performed with his partner Kyle Gass. These were some of the earliest shows of their famous group "Tenacious D." Will Farrell was part of a trio called "Simpatico" who wore unitards in primary colors and did loosely choreographed tumbling and erratic dances. Jay Johnston and Paul F. Tompkins did their sketch as two men from the company "Tintrell." They were both in suit and tie with briefcases doing a boasting sales pitch with rapid-fire description of the product where it was impossible to know what the product actually was. Greg Behrendt was perfecting his morning dj asshole character. Another comic did stand-up after I did my word salad performance art comedy. She called me "art school" derisively. I was so earnest and new to the scene that even the smallest slight cut me to the core. I don't know what I expected people to think of what I was doing. Her calling it "art school" was accurate and direct and not necessarily even an insult. Bob Odenkirk did stand-up. People weren't famous yet. Bob had some notoriety from being a writer on SNL. I remember Molly Shannon passing out flyers to everyone she came in contact with, smiling, "Come to my one-woman show! You'll love it. It's going to be so much fun!"

I started to experiment more on stage. One of my favorite bits I used to do was to let the emcee announce me and not come out. The idea that I was performing and I didn't want to be on stage was hilarious to me. Another gag I used to do was to take the hugest pratfall on my way up to the stage after my name was announced.

"I really wish I could perform for you tonight, but I really can't be here. I have jury duty tomorrow and really bad hair plus I've got to call my mother. Besides, I'm not really equipped to perform. I don't really have the skills to speak in front of people. It was never nurtured in me; I used to be ambidextrous when I was in kindergarten. They beat it out of me. Which hand do you write with? The right or the left? Pick one! So, I don't have that skill anymore. I used to be a smoker. I was really good at it as a baby. At eight months old, I would crawl over to my uncle's smoking table and grab the cigarettes and start puffing away! Everyone freaked out. 'No! No! Babies don't smoke.' So now I don't have that skill anymore. It would've probably come in handy with some of my acting auditions. I was also a really good lover as a baby. Apparently, I would go up to other babies and try to get it on with them. I had all the moves. As a toddler, I tried out some stripper moves on my cousin Kevin, grinding, pumping my hips, gritting my teeth together, pursing my lips, grabbing my own hair, touching my own ass—I guess you get the idea. Anyway, my family freaked out. My aunt said, 'Look what she's doing, somebody stop her, it's disgusting.' So yeah. I'm not a great lover. Completely frigid. I kiss with my mouth all tight and shut. Losing this ability has caused me to lose a lot of relationships."

I would go on about how my parents didn't pay attention to me, and continue to show what types of stuff I would do if I were to perform. I started doing bits from an old Joan Rivers act, not telling people what it was:

"The nose on him. Who's the one with the nose? Rod Stewart, if he had a drug problem, he would inhale half of Manhattan. Stevie Wonder, that poor son of a bitch, would someone tell him he's wearing a macramé plant holder on his head?" I would then play a recording of the Joan Rivers bits with the audience laughing uproariously and then tell the audience that they weren't really ready for comedy anyway.

The audience may not have been getting it, but my friends did. They were my support system and barometer of what was good. They were receptive to my style of comedy and experimentation and I looked up to them. I was at the beginning of finding my voice comedically. I had finally found a real group of friends and creative peers.

I was even rescued from my living situation. Tracy Katsky, a native Los Angeleno and aspiring TV exec, had a roommate who was moving out. Sarah Silverman was moving from New York to be her new roommate. Tracy said she would ask Sarah if I could stay with them. Sarah agreed and I lived in their living room for two years. We made actual food and hung out with each other. Sarah ran jokes past me. Tracy and I made art and listened to music for hours. Tracy suggested that I do a one-woman show.

"Really?"

"Yes. You should do a one-woman show."

I had gained a reputation for my unexpected performances. My off-the-cuff delivery and commitment to being in the moment were fun to watch. There was genuine excitement in the scene for the one-woman show I was going to do. All my friends came out and word spread about it. I pulled out all of my favorite scraps of paper and some markers and spread out on the floor. It was disjointed and unmemorized, but I threw it up on stage at a place called Luna Park in West Hollywood, adjacent to American Burgers and the car wash (it was also across the street from The Abbey, a high-octane gay bar). My show didn't have a name, but I wore my uniform from the Hard Rock Cafe where I was a waitress. I would crown myself onstage as "Best Waitress" and take questions from the audience that I had previously passed out.

"What's the secret ingredient of the Hard Rock n' Roll Chili?"

"I'm so glad you asked!"

The managers who owned Ramon's house were in the audience. They didn't sign me that night, but I would end up being one of their clients as a comedic actress. It was beginning to look like the start of my life.

# GOLDEN GLOBES

If you would have told me that being invited to the Golden Globes contained an element of humiliation, I wouldn't have believed you. Until it happened to me. I was informed that I was invited but without a plus one. Which meant to me, "You're invited. Barely." I was determined not to let going alone ruin the magic of the evening. But sometimes, even when you're determined, you still fail.

I told myself, *You're going alone, but you're not going to be alone once you get there*. This was incorrect.

I took in the scenery. It was so exciting just to be there. The ambience was upscale, romantic, and fun. I was the first one seated at one of the most beautifully set tables I'd ever seen. So elegant. Flowers, a gold-lined plate on top of another gold-lined plate, real crystal glassware. So many forks. Why three? There was a card with my name on it. I looked at the other name cards expecting to see a coworker's name, a fellow actor from *24*. The rest of the name cards were people from another show, called *Ugly Betty*. That wasn't even the same genre as *24*. I'm first to a table where I'm sitting with

people I don't know, from a show I don't watch or work on. I took
a deep breath and put a positive spin on the situation telling myself,
*They're actors, they'll be fun!*

I ordered a drink and tried to relax. No one said hello or made
eye contact. I got through that first drink and still no one showed
up to the table. I ordered another. Halfway through my second
drink, I got up and looked over the balcony.

My table was on the mezzanine. When I looked down, I could
see all of the other more important tables close to the stage. I spot-
ted Kiefer and the producers of our show. I yelled down, "Hey
guys!" They didn't hear me. I tried to go down to say hello but was
blocked by security. On my way back up to the mezzanine I was
feeling buzzed and emotional. Another wave of humiliation came
over me. Then I realized the bar was on the mezzanine. Easy. I
don't even need to go back to the table—I can hang out and mingle
at the bar.

I passed Puff Daddy, who did a double take when he saw me.
"That's my girl! Chloe O'Brian!" We did a fist bump, which I was
not entirely adept at. But I was overjoyed by the attention. This
is what I'm talking about! We got some action. Next, I saw Sheryl
Crow and I know her, so I walked toward her. She was standing
with Courteney Cox. As soon as they were close enough, I blurted,
"I feel so alone!" Sheryl didn't miss a beat and concurred, "Yes, I
always feel awkward at these things."

Courteney Cox just screwed up her face at me like a stinky
princess who was too good to acknowledge me. Then, I realized
that I actually did not know Sheryl Crow. I had just listened to
her music and watched her videos. I laughed as if I was making a
hilarious joke and turned away from them, looking for Puff Daddy.
He was busy.

I came to the conclusion that I had experienced enough for one night and it was time to show myself out. I made my way out of the bar, down a hallway, through a dirty service area into a parking lot where a mob of people pushed each other to get the attention of the valet. It was cold and a guy in a suit pushed in front of me to go first. The construct of glamour took another hit that night as the reality of what this was sunk in: This event was great if you were famous enough and even better if you were winning an award. If you weren't one or both of those things, it's more likely that you were having an extremely mediocre to terrible time in very uncomfortable clothing.

Disclosures: I've been in a Sheryl Crow music video but I still don't know her. I was also at the Golden Globes another year when *24* won. Completely different experience: Everyone was together, I got to go on the stage when we received the award, pop champagne, and do photos and party afterward. But when you're not winning or popular, you're not having a good time. That's the moral of this story. Also, I did not get my own Golden Globe—I'm not sure who took it home.

# MY WORST AUDITION BESIDES THE ONE WHERE I WAS DRUNK

I never thought this was a position I'd be in and here I was auditioning for a real TV show! I was more nervous than I thought I would be, which was annoying. I kept telling myself, "Get it together!"

I waited in a hallway on a metal folding chair with the audition material on three pieces of paper that lay on my lap. I was surrounded by other women also auditioning for the part of the nervous secretary. I saw Paget Brewster. Later, she would become a friend, but in that moment I caught a glimpse of the most beautiful, stylish, perfect woman—and my competition. I wasn't just jealous, I was defensive about it. I didn't understand how she could have clothes and accessories and be so beautiful, charming, and funny. I tried to look good for the audition. The concept of having a cute outfit was beyond me. My normal outfit was black Doc Martens boots, cargo shorts, an oversized T-shirt, and suspenders to hold the pants up. On this day, I borrowed a girly blouse, paired it with Dickies brand work pants, and wore some baby barrettes in my hair. I rocked some blue eyeliner and earrings that hung down. This said "professional."

*It's a fluke I'm here, it doesn't mean anything.* That's what I told myself. The trick was to cover up that you cared too much. I didn't understand why my heart was beating faster, why I was sweating, and why I started to question my looks and weight. *There's nothing I can do now.* I would just have to go into the room and go for it. I told myself it would be fun.

When it was my turn, I read for the part and everything fell into place. My nervousness transformed into comedy, and I surprised myself by my own natural rhythm and ability to create a character in the room. I knew I did a good job, I could feel it. I was happy with myself for being able to deliver.

I was told I did so well that the producers wanted to see me in an hour. I did not know what that meant. The casting people were the gatekeepers for the producers who were the gatekeepers for the network. Getting the part would depend on hitting the right chord with each group. You had to be the flavor of the moment. Embody a certain something that would excite all of these people at the same time and in the same way. Or the person with the most power would have to like you the best and fight for you. This seemed like a largely arbitrary and very silly way to get a job. It was a lottery of making a good impression based on something completely subjective, and the senselessness of it all was really appealing.

However, once through the first round and into the smaller pool of the lottery (for the pilot that would be made but most likely never even get on the air), my nervousness went up a level. I was shaking. I didn't know I was capable of being as nervous as I was.

When I got into the room this time, the producers were there. About five guys dressed nicely. Directly across from me was

Meredith Baxter Birney. It was her show and I was auditioning to play the nervous secretary in her network television pilot. She was an icon. Television royalty. I had no idea she would be there. The veil had been lifted and I was seeing someone in the flesh I had idolized as a child.

She played Elyse Keaton, the liberal hippie mom of Alex P. Keaton, her young Republican son on *Family Ties*. I had watched her come to life on my TV screen for so many episodes in the living room and kitchen of the fictional house I loved. This was too much for my already thin grasp on my composure. I lost it. I didn't cry, but words stopped coming out of my mouth. I briefly blacked out and I tried to power through but the words were skipping, jumping, and stuttering through my lips. My brain was forcing me to act normal and my body wasn't having it.

Then I looked directly into her eyes. She felt so bad for me, I could see it on her face. This made me feel worse. The look in her eyes was begging me not to "go there." Elyse Keaton wanted me to get it together. But it was too late. I went there, briefly blacking out.

Being able to perform with ease was no longer an option. I could only hear a high-pitch sound in my ears, I knew my voice was doing something but I wasn't sure what, I began to feel faint. Then, somehow, I got up and walked out of the room. I didn't get the part.

This was the beginning of what would become a lifetime of auditions. The special feeling of putting time, energy, and emotional investment in something that amounts to a crapshoot. Even if I did the best I could, of course, the decision is arbitrary and based on what others think they want in the moment. This was also the first of what was about to become many encounters with famous people. It was appropriate that the first time was auditioning in front of was a mother figure to me growing up. *Please choose me, approve of me, I'm not good enough!* My inner monologue did its magic, driving me forward trying to fill a need that would never fully be met with any part. This was the beginning of my new life, a rite of passage into a lifelong career of being a professional actor and comedian. This experience was the first feather in my professional actor hat.

# PIMP KEVIN

You never know exactly when it's going to be, the day you meet your pimp. I wasn't ready. I didn't know how much my pussy would be worth. Or what people would want my body for. But the universe doesn't give you anything you can't handle. When life gives you a glimpse of your potential, do you rise up and meet the moment or do you run away?

I was walking down the streets of East LA in my favorite uniform of pajama bottoms, a large men's T-shirt, a backpack, headphones, and plastic mirrored sunglasses from the gas station. I was in my twenties. I hung out with my friends in bars at night—getting up by eleven A.M. was an early start. Most likely I was taking a nice long walk to get coffee. Wandering around aimlessly is a favorite pastime of mine. For as much success as I was having acting, I didn't act like it. As I was passing by Tang's 24 Hour Donuts, a now-faded, once brightly colored establishment from the 1970s, a young woman called out to me.

"Hey!" She seemed to know me. I turned to look. "Hey, what's up?"

"Nothing." I found myself engaging with her like we were old friends because she wanted me to. It felt like I owed her something.

"How's it going?" Her tone suggested she had missed me and was glad I was back. I was searching her face for some recognition. Nope, definitely did not know her. She had a vacant look in her eyes but her voice was so casual and friendly. She had very short shorts on. Her skin was so white it was nearly translucent. Everything about her was pale. Her shorts were pale blue. She had pale bruises on her pale legs. I surmised that she was certainly not the type of girl I would hang out with or even ordinarily be in a position to meet. She seemed like a wet noodle. Clearly we had nothing in common. I was a wet noodle on the move.

"It's going good."

"Are you going downtown?" *No, I wasn't going downtown, but I could be! How did she know?*

She asked if I was taking the bus. This was fun. Where was she going with this conversation? I "yes anded" her like in improv class! I really thought she was going to try to sell me drugs.

"Oh, cool. Are you looking for work?" *I'm recurring on the Kirstie Alley sitcom* Veronica's Closet *and waiting to see if my sketch comedy pilot is getting picked up by the network.*

"Yes and . . ."

"Well, I might have something for you. Come this way."

We walked into Tang's 24 Hour Donuts. As soon as she walked in the door, there was a synchronized movement that had nothing to do with doughnuts. The boy behind the counter whispered to a man who went into the back. There was another girl who looked down and scooted outside. A secret operation of some sort was afoot. My girl led me to the outdoor formica picnic table where an unsmiling man in sunglasses sat under a pink metal umbrella. Then she made herself scarce.

His stature was foreboding. It was almost high noon and he was wearing a North Face ski jacket in ninety-degree weather. He had on large gold chains. Who is this guy?

"Christine says you're looking for work."

"Oh, yeah . . ."

"I might be able to help you. We're doing really well out here." *Doing well with what?*

"Oh—"

"These are all my girls. I take care of them."

"You do?"

"I could take care of you too. We have a few girls who are doing really well." *Doing well, how?* Money. They're making money. He wants me to join the team. I could be doing well too. Will I be selling my genitals? When I met Pimp Kevin, it ignited a sense of possibility.

This is when I learned that I'm pretty enough to be a lady of the night. I would have dressed differently if I'd known I was going to meet my prospective pimp. He didn't come out and say it. That's how they do it without getting caught! They just talk around it.

"Have a seat." He tried to get the upper hand.

"I'm good." Uh-oh. He didn't like me not following his orders. My heart was beating so fast. I did not want to sit across from this guy, but I really wanted to know what happens next. Does this lady become a ho or what?

"Lift up your sunglasses, let me see your eyes." He wants to check the goods. I left my body and watched myself from above as I lifted my sunglasses.

"Do you have a boyfriend? If you have a boyfriend, you can't be living with him." I had been living with my boyfriend for two years.

"No . . ." That seemed like the correct answer.

"Good. Do you have a car?"

"No." *Don't tell him about my brand-new iced-teal Honda civic!*

"Good. It's better if you don't."

"Do you have a pimpmobile?"

"What you say?"

"I saw this documentary . . . never mind."

"What's your name?"

"Mary."

"Mary. I can help you and you can help me." Holy shit. I could become a real prostitute today.

"You can help me?"

"Yes, I understand the woman's condition." Maybe I would finally be taken care of! I was too scared. My adrenaline kicked in—I had to get out of there but also not make a fuss. I took two steps backward.

"Oh OK. I'll think about it."

"What's your phone number?"

"I don't know *your* name," I hedged.

"Kevin, but they call me Lawrence." Why is this pimp named Lawrence? There must be something I don't understand culturally.

"What's your phone number?" he pressed.

"Well, you know, I'm not sure . . ."

I moved sideways toward the door, steady in my speed as to not anger the beast. He asked one more time.

"I am going to keep thinking about it."

"I think you have thought about it." Oh shit. The clincher. He was trying to seal the deal.

That was how he was going to get me into his grubby hands and cart me around like his prized possession, like a low-grade princess. I don't have bruises all over my legs yet like Christine does. I'll never be that skinny either, but maybe I'd be the cushiony prostitute.

I replied, "I'll think about it some more, OK? Thanks a lot. I'll see you later."

I slowly backed out as if I was at a cocktail party and had to use the restroom and ran down the street away from the scene as fast as I could.

I told my boyfriend. He was not very happy with me. "Why would you do that? You put yourself in so much danger." *Did I?*

"I don't know!" I felt belittled.

"I can't believe you! How could you do this?" He stormed off. What's his deal? This is how I have a good time. I thought he loved my curious nature and ability to put myself in new situations. He doesn't get me.

I was worried that Lawrence was following me. For weeks afterward, I avoided the entire two-mile radius of Tang's. I kept looking over my shoulder to see if Lawrence was about to drag me off the street and put me on, well, the street. Thankfully, he never found me. I never saw Christine again and I never had a donut from Tang's.

# GETTING THE PART

Sometimes hanging out leads to work. I was given the part on *24* because the executive producer, Joel Surnow, had seen me playing an overbearing sister in *Punch-Drunk Love*, a film starring Adam Sandler and Emily Watson, written and directed by Paul Thomas Anderson. Paul Anderson used to hang out at a club called Largo in Los Angeles. Largo was an intimate supper club, and it was the place to be if you were a comedian, musician, or writer. The audience was discerning and forgiving. It was a great place to experiment and be vulnerable, and those two things were my middle name. I was lucky enough to have this be my hangout for quite a few years. I performed there regularly and dated a musician who was friends with Paul, so he was familiar with me as a person and a performer. One night we were all laughing backstage and there was this motorcycle helmet and jumpsuit. I was getting ready to go on stage for my comedy set, and they dared me to put the jumpsuit and helmet on apropos of nothing. It was silly and us just goofing around. That's the type of thing he had seen me do, not exactly nuanced acting.

Paul had written *Punch-Drunk Love* and Adam Sandler was already attached. He asked me if I would come over to Adam's house and read through some scenes with them as one of the sisters of Adam's character, Barry. When he asked, I assumed that it was for his creative purposes to see if he liked the way the scene was flowing. He wanted me to do him a solid and read it with Adam so that they could hear the material. I didn't realize that this was his way of auditioning me for the part. I didn't dare consciously assume that it was—I was just happy to have the opportunity to be in their company.

I went to Adam's house in the San Fernando Valley. We sat on white wrought-iron furniture at a small table with an umbrella on the lawn in the backyard. I read through a few scenes with Adam and then left. It was surreal. A few days later, Paul asked if I wanted to play the part and soon after that I was reading with the other sisters for their auditions! So, that casual read-through *was* my audition. I was very grateful and excited. I had a part in a Paul Thomas Anderson movie!

During the filming, I remember sitting outside with Emily Watson, who plays Adam's love interest in the movie. We both had on long puffy winter coats that were borrowed from wardrobe, and we were drinking Cokes on a bench next to each other, giggling. That's the weird thing about acting. Here I was sitting next to this amazing actress, whom I knew from the harrowing 1996 movie *Breaking the Waves*, directed by Lars von Trier. Her performance in that movie shook me to the core and stayed with me for weeks after. I had never seen a character that was so emotionally nuanced and disturbed. Someone that you rooted for but wished would become more stable, yet you knew they wouldn't. It was like watching an emotional car wreck and you couldn't look away. She was nominated for an Oscar for her performance in this film. When I met her, she could not have been more down-to-earth and easy to be around. We only spent a number of days together. She was humble and funny and someone I will most likely never see again. The fact that she was so easy to be around speaks volumes about her character, and I also got a boost of confidence being in the presence of greatness.

The main character, Barry, had six more sisters that needed to be cast. Paul used women who were really sisters and not actors. They were very loud and outgoing. I remember sitting for a scene at a dinner table. Emily and I (the professional performers) quietly waited in between takes while the non-actors yelled and laughed and couldn't have been more comfortable making the set their own. They were so raucous that they had to be interrupted by the assistant director and told it was time to shoot.

One of my biggest scenes was shot in the San Fernando Valley in a warehouse that was set as Barry's workplace. He had his own business selling novelty items. He wore a bright blue suit. Elizabeth, his sister (me), wants him to have a girlfriend, get married, and have kids. She is not happy with what she perceives as Barry not being willing to put himself out there for love. She thinks his life is passing him by and he's not trying. She storms into his work to inform him that she has set him up on a date with one of her friends from work. We have a conversation where I'm pressing him to give me answers about his dating life and he doesn't want to be talking.

The scene was a minute or two of dialogue and we shot it around thirty times. That's a bit much if you ask me, but no one was asking me, and my job was to act. So I did, over and over and over. Many months later, Paul wasn't happy with the colors in the warehouse and so we did reshoots. I couldn't believe he rented the building again, brought back set designers, actors, the camera department, and so on, just because he didn't like the colors. This is the thing I most admire about him: Not only is he insanely talented and smart but he believes in himself so much, he creates his own reality. If you're on a Paul Anderson set, the most important thing is his vision. His artistic process is given precedent above everything else. His love for his craft trickles down to every department. Everyone who works with him has respect for his process and vision, and that is a very rare and special thing to be a part of.

Adam Sandler's role was very different from anything he had done up to that time. The character of Barry is neurotic, in pain, and has extreme social anxiety—not exactly your usual characteristics for a romantic lead or a man known for comedy. The movie was not a smash hit. I believe that Adam's fans weren't ready to see him playing a serious role that involved real emotional pain. They wanted the larger-than-life goofy guy. *Punch-Drunk Love* does have a happy ending, but the journey to get there is very anxiety inducing.

One person who did see the movie was Joel Surnow, the executive producer of the hit TV show *24*. My agent called and said, "They want to see you for this show." I told her no because I had just had an audition for *CSI* as Rape Victim Number Two and it was a really bad experience. My agent said, "They really want to see you for this. The part isn't written but they said they are thinking of developing it." Oh great, when they say they're going to possibly develop, that's their way of getting you in there for a two-line part. No thank you. My agent said, "I really think you should go in on this, they really like you. I'm going to send you a few episodes of the show to watch so you can be familiar with it."

So I went. It was far away and it was a hundred degrees outside in June. The casting office was way outside of LA in this warehouse. When I was walking down the hall to the audition room, three guys were walking toward me. One of the executive producers was talking to me. He would change my life forever. "We're so glad you could come. We're big fans of yours. You're so talented!"

"Thank you." He introduced me to the other producers and we went into a casting room.

"You were in *Punch-Drunk Love*. What's it like to work with PTA? And your boyfriend is the composer? Wow, what's it like to be around and have so much talent?" I laughed uncomfortably. Is this guy for real? He seemed super genuine.

He continued, "There's nothing on the page. We haven't written this part yet. But we want you to do it. We're going to write more for this character. It's an agent at the counter-terrorist unit. A real techie person who works on the computer."

"Oh OK, thank you. That's really nice. I have never done a drama like this."

"We know. We think you'll be great. Are you a fan of the show?"

"Yes, for sure."

"You don't watch the show, do you?"

"No." They all laughed. "My agent sent me a few episodes to watch and it's really good but no, I haven't seen all the episodes." I left the meeting feeling like I was floating on a cloud. I didn't believe anything would come of this, but I felt seen by people in the business. I felt validated. This meeting alone would give me the energy to keep going for a few months. Then something remarkable happened. They hired me!

My first contract was for four episodes, for a small amount of money. *24* was already a huge hit when I started. My first scene was with Kiefer Sutherland. His character, Jack Bauer, is undercover and in order to get tight with some terrorists he gets mildly addicted to heroin. My character barges into his office to tell him about a technical problem that is affecting my ability to do my work.

Included in my first line was lots of computer jargon that I didn't understand, but I got the gist of the emotional undertone enough to know how I wanted to play it. His character snaps at me, yelling to leave him alone. I have another emphatic line about whatever was happening that needed attention. He yells at me more and I leave his office.

I was startled by his intensity but made it through the first couple of takes. I felt pretty good. No one gave notes or said anything was wrong, which is usually a good sign. Then there was a thirty-minute break while they relit the room for the next angle of the scene. When we started again, I began my line, but the end where all the jargon was had disappeared from my mind entirely. The more I tried to retrieve it, the worse it got. I began to sweat; the flow of the scene with my gaff was becoming tedious. Kiefer, the director, and the entire crew had no choice but to wait for me to get the line. I didn't. We had to take a break. I ran off set, grabbed a script, and went into a corner and began to say the lines over and over. Ten minutes later, we tried the scene again and I made it through. The next time there was a break, I spent it drilling the lines over and over. None of my previous jobs required a lot of studying to learn the lines, and I have an adverse reaction to hard work.

That night I spent my time making sure to know my lines for the next day inside and out. The next morning I showed up sheepishly, embarrassed at my previous bombastic "I know what I'm doing" casual attitude when clearly I was in over my head. The director saw my body language and put his hand on my shoulder laughing. "Don't worry, that happens to everyone on the first day." I was so relieved that I wasn't the only one who bungled the lines and froze up trying to get used to the frenetic pace of the dialogue, especially with long breaks in between.

My four episodes turned into four more and then six episodes, and so on. The feedback about my character was that she was weird and annoying. Around a year after I showed up, they started to write me as being loyal and helpful to Jack Bauer. My character had dimension and helped the hero of the show. It was a very smart choice by the writers, and it was further fueled by my comedic delivery. It created a unique, unexpected character. This was a very fortuitous turn in my life.

Three years into appearing on the show, I was asked to be a series regular. No longer would I need to worry if they were going to pick me up for more episodes. Now the worry would be if the show would be picked up. The show was such a huge hit, it was assumed it would come back, but we never knew for sure.

It was time to admit to myself that I was a professional actor. I did this for a living. I had to step into my own shoes and accept that I was a recognizable character from people's favorite TV show. I was on a hit drama on network television starring alongside Kiefer Sutherland who I knew from all his movies, which I watched as a kid back in Michigan. If I tried to figure out how this happened it would be too much for my brain. It wasn't in the description of the possibilities on offer to me when I was growing up. There was nothing in that description except marry your high school sweetheart and work at Olive Garden.

When young actors ask me for advice on how to get into acting, I say, "Perform as much as possible," which is what I genuinely do believe. My fearlessness as a performer got me to Los Angeles. My ability to throw myself into situations and follow what I liked to do helped me to get seen by people who were willing to give me a chance to work as an actor. If you're willing to deal with a lot of anxiety and a lifetime of instability, you should definitely take this advice.

# THE DAY THE ROMANCE DIED

In the seventh grade, my friend and I planned a Valentine's Day party while our pre-teen hormones raged. I was ready to find true love and a romance that would whisk me off my feet to be adored and kissed by a handsome male suitor. No more making out with pillowcases and pretending they were Indiana Jones. It was time for real boys and we were going to be proactive, so my friend Julie and I planned a Valentine's Day party that would take place in my parents' basement. We made a meticulous list of boys and girls in our class. We wrote out invitations in our best cursive and made heart decorations with red construction paper, carefully tracing the edges with glue and iridescent glitter, and hung them from the ceiling using red ribbon. The basement was transformed into a romantic dance floor. We put up twinkle lights and fired up the jam box to play Madonna and Atlantic Starr.

The party planning was the best part. The dreaming and the decorating. The rest was downhill. I did make out with a boy but he wasn't who I wanted. I remember dancing with him and then him sticking his tongue in my mouth. It was salty because he was also eating McDonald's french fries. Why couldn't the cute quiet one, Charles, want to dance with me?

Because my expectations weren't met in a situation that was mostly out of my control, instead of adjusting or maybe gaining a communication skill or realizing this had nothing to do with me, I blamed myself: *What were you thinking planning a party to get a boyfriend? You can't do that!* I was also ashamed of the guy who liked me. I took it as a measurement of my own attractiveness. I wasn't good enough to get the good guys. I've held this idea my entire life. It was how I felt inside and then I used outside experiences to reinforce this idea. This obviously was not fair to me or him. He didn't know. His name was Darryl. He was a loud redhead with freckles who went for it. If I were him, why wouldn't I try to make out with me and eat fries?! This guy was amazing, revolutionary maybe.

My next opportunity for love came at an unexpected time and in a very unromantic way. It was a little later, when I was in the eighth grade. I didn't know him but I knew his name. Will Dumetz. On this particular day, Will Dumetz appeared out of the bushes to walk me home. His face was acne scarred, his eyes were squinty, and his hair was white blond. His tall frame was shaped like a question mark. He used his height to lurk rather than stand. I recognized him as that guy who got high and skipped school. He was too quiet and seemed like he could lash out at any moment. His entire body was suppressing his inner rage. His walk was contrived and pent up, like someone trying to "walk normal," but it came out in a stilted swagger. With all of this as my impression of him, I still didn't have the awareness to get away from him. Then again, I was walking by myself; there was nowhere to get away to.

On this particular day, he and his weird swagger decided to walk me home. He chose me to follow, to talk to. Why was he giving me attention? Maybe he needed someone to be kind to him. I didn't know he knew I existed, but today he was looking at me, playing the part of a shy guy. Maybe I misunderstood him and he wanted someone to talk to, someone who would listen to him. I wanted to ask, "Where did you come from? How do you even know me? Why do you want to walk me home?" Instead, I allowed him to steer a very minimal conversation about who each of us knew at school and who we had in common. Then there were a lot of awkward silences. I noticed he was smiling for no reason and laughing a little. He seemed nervous. I was flattered. There was a chance that if I got real, Will Dumetz and I could have a connection, so I told him that my aunt just died—you know, to set up trust in a relationship, you start by revealing inappropriate information to someone you just met. I distinctly remember him doing a bad impression of someone who cares. I felt like a fool for saying it out loud to him but it also felt good to say it. Because my aunt did just die and I remember my cousins in a hugging circle of grief standing in the mausoleum a few minutes after her burial. I needed to talk to someone about it. He was not the person.

This did not lead to a connection but it did lead us to his cousin Tal's house. Tal was my friend. He was not home. "Where's Tal?" I asked.

"I don't know but let's go hang out in the hammock."

Then his large body was on top of me while he made out with me. I couldn't move. It was not enjoyable or wanted. I didn't know how to understand a potential threat. If someone wanted to talk to me and was acting mostly reasonable, I thought I had to go along with it, that it was my duty to be polite.

When his body was on top of mine, I was afraid he wouldn't stop. I was in no way thinking about sex. I didn't understand what it was, and I wasn't ready to understand what it was. So the forcefulness, the pressure, the weight, the strength, the physical touching was something I had maybe seen in a movie, but in my mind it was supposed to be romantic and consensual. This was something I didn't know existed.

There was the one time that the neighbor boy kept tackling me and shoving leaves down my shirt. Or the few moments my brother-in-law lifted me up and threw me in the pool and his hands went over my chest when I was too old to play that game. So this was that. But it was the next step. I was thinking, *Will he hurt me? How quickly can I get out from underneath him, without pissing him off?*

Eventually Will Dumetz allowed me to wrangle myself out from beneath his weight. I walked home. He is a ghost to me now. This memory of him was one of my first experiences of sexual intimacy, and it is part of a composite that informed me of how men behave. It was deeply disappointing, jarring, and shame inducing. It was even further from the couple's dance in my parents' basement but, similarly, I construed it as my own fault. I could have and should have gotten myself away from him earlier, but I'm glad I had that experience and that it wasn't worse. It taught me what could happen. This interaction has lived in me my whole life as light trauma. This is part of life. Like a toddler touching a hot stove, now I knew.

In my twenties, having no idea what healthy boundaries were and with a sexual drive to be validated and desired, I would make myself available to guys. Still using that concept of "the good listener" that I thought would get me to a mutual understanding with Will Dumetz, I was able now to use it to get guys to fall in love with me. At the end of the day, no matter how much I convinced myself that I was in love too, it was really about how much I could validate their behavior and get some nuggets of attention in return. This was a type of relationship I engaged in again and again. I would fall hard into love, and once I was no longer able to be a good listener, once I started to no longer be able to deny my own needs, I would fall out of love and break their hearts. This was a terrible model but it was still much better than having assault be the beginning of a relationship.

I'm on a new road now, of beginning to understand what I like and who I am. It's the start of beginning to believe in romance again. The romance I'm looking for now has nothing to do with candles and wine but the ability to be completely self-possessed. I guess it's falling in love with myself and having hopes that a partner will someday be interested enough to ride along with me.

# BLACK DILDO

There's a moment in every relationship when you look back and think, *Oh,* that *was the moment it all fell apart. That was the thing that we never recovered from.* The event itself can be retold at parties, but the larger wordless embarrassment of thinking this was a lifelong partnership would linger with me for years.

Six years into the relationship, did I question the sex? Not really. I mean, I knew Max liked to be tightly wrapped around me while falling asleep. I marveled at his cuddle ability. I would qualify it as too much cuddling. I tried to appreciate it because it's usually the guy who wants no part of cuddling. Well, this one took spooning to the next level. Everyone knows you cuddle for a few minutes until rolling to your side of the bed. What he did was more of a clutching. I marveled at how his arm wouldn't fall asleep and he would wait it out as long as he could. It was annoying and suffocating, but I tried to convince myself that this was a guy who is not afraid to show love.

What was he trying to hold on to? *If I squeeze you hard enough, it is intimacy. I don't need to address my desires and true thoughts and feelings about myself, I'll just hold on to your body and this will replace actual communication. Squeeze. You're my everything, I'm so in love with you.* The clutching represented what he was willing to be true in his daytime life. The life that he told everyone about: *I have a girlfriend. We are in love. We are the cornerstone of our social scene. Everyone loves us.* I believed him. The truth was secret, hidden beneath the clutching. Perhaps his truth ran rampant in his dreams and he thought if he held on to my female body, his unconscious would get the message that he loved vaginas the most.

Max and I had been together a couple of years when I orchestrated the purchase of the dilapidated house we lived in. I had money saved up from my various acting jobs in the late nineties. He was successful but had no interest in being domestic and establishing roots. I pushed for that to happen because we were in love and we wanted to couple up for life. This was our house. We bought it together. It wasn't some transitory apartment. It was our house, in which to consummate our love. A fixer-upper that we would spend our lives remodeling and decorating with artifacts from our travels abroad. When I found this craftsman in West Hollywood that was falling apart, occupied by a hoarder and his lover who kept many cats in the front room, I knew we had to have it. This was before I discovered my habit of making assumptions about my partners, not realizing I was the one making the decisions while they went along with whatever I pushed for. It would be our DIY love haven. I thought we would redo it together in an eclectic design. I would excitedly talk about all of the vintage furniture we could get and the wood chips we could use to cover the entire front yard. He gave no indication that he would be participating in any way. I don't know why I thought a guy who had lived in transient hotels and on other people's couches and took cabs instead of purchasing a car would suddenly be interested in creating a home. He did like material things and contributed to the household financially. He just had no interest in having a home. I was the one who made it happen.

When we first started dating and I got a glimpse of his room, I gasped. It was very dusty and dark. His mattress was on the floor, with no sheets. It was shabby and stained, surrounded by piles of coins from night after night of him emptying his pockets onto the floor. *I don't know if I can do this.* He wore the same three pairs of boxers that were threadbare. But he was a brilliant painter who knew about the Dada and Fluxus movements. This is what sold me on moving forward with the relationship, that and my desperate desire to be around someone considered to be a creative genius. *He's allowing me into his world. He has blind spots in a lot of normal areas of life because he is so talented in others. He can't live by normal rules.* (Thank god that included not believing in marriage. I wanted it but he would not budge. I'm so glad he didn't. That would have been the worst decision of my life.) He loved to talk about art and history. These were all things that I didn't have any practice at talking about, so I was in awe. When I would make one comment to his ten and he listened, I was on top of the world. Max liked to shop for antique photographs and artifacts from the Civil War era. In the moment, he would be so excited with his purchase, then, one by one the photos and objects would get put in his office and never removed from the bag he brought them home in. He loved diners and cafés, sitting in front of a cup of coffee for hours on end stoking his creativity. I thought he was a renaissance man, an artist shaping the modern landscape. The depth of his pretentiousness wouldn't occur to me until years later. What I thought was creative genius was a guy hell-bent on pretending to be self-aware while in reality he was not able to discover who he really was, a guy who couldn't express his real nature or desires and instead talked in vague platitudes and refused to really commit to anything in his life.

When Max and I had been in the house for a year, which by this time had been repainted and had a couple of couches in it, I knew something was off. He wasn't in his usual spot on the couch with one of his abstract collages nearby but really he was staring into the TV. It was possible but unlikely that he'd be in his studio (an unfinished bedroom filled with boxes and dust). If he was napping that would not make any sense. He didn't nap in the middle of the day, because he slept late. This was his prime time. I went upstairs. Maybe he's hiding in the overgrown weeds in the backyard. Unless he went on a walk, which he has never done before. He must be in the bedroom. I hope he's OK. As I approached the bedroom door, I saw it was open a crack. I heard blankets rustling and some breathing. What I saw next was not napping. You're thinking I walked in on him cheating on me. What he was actually doing required so much more . . . effort. It took me moments to make a composite of the images and sounds. My brain had to put them together like a puzzle. If he's masturbating, where is the hand? And the penis? This was something else.

Yes, there was masturbating, but not the hand-on-penis kind. He was having anal sex with himself. I saw a black dildo come out and then he put it back up his rear again. I had never before witnessed a loved one in this type of position. I thought my eyes were playing tricks on me. I immediately closed the door and backed out and whispered to myself, "I'll leave you two alone." It was the cartoonishly large black dildo, the one they put at the front of the sex shop just to get your attention. I didn't think anyone really used those, and here was the love of my life very adeptly shoving one in and out of his back door.

He was in the throes of passion with himself and this object. I was supposed to be there for lovemaking. But he didn't want me to be. He had a much more vigorous and intimate sexual relationship without me. It's OK that he liked stuff in his ass. That's a preference. (I've heard it is the first couple of times!) The realization that I didn't really know him and that I wasn't really included in his sexual desires is what really hurt. Yes, I was jealous of his big black dildo.

Days turned into weeks. We weren't having sex and I realized he never talked to me about anything of consequence or value. Things became strained. I started to push him to talk about our relationship in general. I was too scared to bring up the dildo. I started by saying that I didn't feel close to him. He took great offense to this, which I didn't understand. The fact that I didn't see him as a perfect partner in every way was not acceptable to him.

It was easier for him to act like he was being attacked. He became the ultimate victim. It was a missed opportunity to directly confront and work through the issue and come out the other side as better people and a stronger couple. Instead of being willing to have a conversation or even an argument, he chose to leave the house. I wanted to have a difficult conversation, and he decided to go to a hotel and never speak to me again.

I was responsible for cleaning out the house by myself and selling it. A comic friend helped me dump the picnic table off a second-story balcony into the backyard to have the trash man pick it up. I also somehow cleaned out the refrigerator that was filled with ants because we had moved out of the house and the power had been off. I got in contact with a real estate agent. Ironically, he was a very well put together gay man who took pity on me. It's like he subconsciously knew about the black dildo. I begged him to sell the house for me. He was busy and thought it would be too hard to get a decent price for it but he did it anyway. It was barely in better shape than when we got it the year before. The front yard was one-fourth filled with wood chips. I pulled all of the weeds and dumped eight bags of wood chips, which didn't make a dent in how many wood chips I would have needed to cover the yard, and was so exhausted from doing it alone.

I was shunned from the social circle we shared. Immediately after the breakup, I continued to go to the bar we hung out at constantly. A week after the breakup, people were avoiding me, so I found myself sitting at the bar talking to the bartender more than usual. She kept giving me sad eyes and then finally she said, "He's talking about you," gesturing to the office. The 'head bartender' was one of my best friends, or so I thought. "It's bad. The things he's saying are really bad. He's calling you nasty names, saying you're crazy, and saying he wants to ruin your career." She had tears in her eyes. I was not able to believe in that moment how bad it could be. Her face pleaded for me to understand.

"Thanks for telling me that."

"I thought you should know."

So, people weren't avoiding me because they were uncomfortable and giving me privacy. It was because the word on the street was that I abruptly broke his heart in a cruel and savage way. In fact, I ran into the sound guy for the club at Coffee Bean & Tea Leaf and started chatting to him like I normally would, and he gave me a dirty look followed by a scolding: "You really broke his heart. How could you do that?" This was so wildly inaccurate, but it was the narrative that he wanted to tell the world. He was famous in our social scene, so his story was the one that people wanted to believe.

At the time, I tried to talk to the head bartender about it; he acted like ne had no idea what I was talking about or why I would be trying to talk to him. Suddenly, we were no longer friends. He treated me like I was acting crazy. It was gaslighting 101. He was able to get me shut out of my own social scene. I had seen him do this to numerous people, but it didn't occur to me how awful it was until it happened to me. I had been around him many times when other people who didn't act the way he wanted got called crazy and unreasonable by him. But I also watched him connect people, foster people's art, and create a place where artists felt safe. When I was in his good graces, I didn't notice all the people he shut out of the club, making it an exclusive place. Every time he gossiped to me about how someone else was crazy, I believed him. Now that it was happening to me, it was shocking to see how quickly people turned on me. I learned that the social circle was never really mine to begin with because their allegiance was to appearance, status, and the scene over real friendship. I was very thankful to the bartender for letting me know what was being said about me and understood I was no longer welcome there.

In response, I acted brash, like I didn't care. I went out partying harder than I ever had for the next two years while my ex was publicly mourning, which was so clownish, but people ate it up with a spoon. I knew he wasn't crying over me—he was crying to look as if he were a person in pain about a breakup. He didn't feel pain over me. His pain was the childhood pain of a little boy who didn't understand his place in the world and never grew up to be a man. His mother never taught him and he didn't know how to teach himself. He only developed ways to act as if he were someone else. A real man would tell his lover about his black dildo, not keep it hidden in the closet. The poor black dildo had to live its life in secret because its owner was ashamed of his desires. The desires were so strong that he had a real habit—I could tell in the three seconds I saw of how he worked that thing. He went to great lengths to behave this way and to keep it hidden. Maybe he wants to do that alone, but I really doubt it. Sex is nicer with two people. The isolation he feels must be so exhausting. Maybe he has told someone by now. I hope so.

I saw him a year later at a party and he was overly enthusiastic about how I was doing and how great it was to see me. I had not one thing to say to him. I fake smiled my way through the conversation. I did learn he had moved into a commercial space above a club and used it as an apartment and took cabs everywhere. I imagined all the take-out boxes, piles of change, and the shabby, thin mattress on the floor and was thankful I got out of that one. He seemed like a very sad person. He still sold paintings and had gallery representation and worked and people were still in awe of his abilities.

Years later, I ran into a woman who worked with him after our breakup, and she told me how much pain he was in and how he cried so much over me. I wonder if he told her about the black dildo that broke *my* heart. Probably not.

# POSTCARDS FROM THE EDGE
# OF THE OUGHTS

It was 2002 and I was living in a terrific duplex on the edge of Culver City. It was a funky old place from the forties. The front room went into a middle room that went into the kitchen that went into the bedroom "galley style," or "shove all the rooms together for the cheapest possible design style." The cabinets had been painted over and over, so there was twenty years of paint. They were chunky cabinets. Good news is, all those layers created an elegant soft close. There was a washer and dryer installed in the kitchen, which was a game changer. It was also cute, clean, and a mile and a half from all the bars I frequented. I had tricked the landlord into picking me, using charm I didn't know I had. My modus operandi was that of a follower. But not anymore. As I stood on the porch with the landlord, I knew I had to turn something on. I wanted nothing less than a handshake deal right then and there that he wouldn't pick anyone else for the place. I tried to ingratiate myself to him by saying, "See those men drag racing up and down this street? I can really relate. I love driving fast."

"Oh yeah?" José didn't know what to make of me.

"Also, nothing says cozy home like whitewashed bars on the doors and windows and concrete in the place where the lawn should be. I love a little lawlessness in the neighborhood. Keeps it interesting." *Oh god. Why can't I stop talking?*

"What?" José said, confused.

"Nothing. Listen, José, I just went through a bad breakup and I don't want to keep looking. Just give me the place."

"I just went through a divorce." Shit just got real. I felt better.

"I knew it. See how much we have in common? You know how I feel going through a terrible breakup and needing a place. Mine was a six-year relationship with a pretentious artist with an inability to experience intimacy who cried like a cartoon baby to anyone who would listen, meanwhile, not having one conversation with me about how to fix it or get closer . . . So, probably similar to your real seventeen-year marriage to a whole woman." It worked. He gave me the place.

I decorated my place very nicely: a bright blue large overstuffed couch from Pottery Barn and a white space age table with one upside-down, funnel-shaped leg holding it up and the prerequisite Indian rug to tie it all together, impressing myself and José, who I kept finding reasons to invite over, but who would never hang out. "José, I think there's a gas leak. Can you come over?" "Hey José, I have some leftover Mongolian barbecue, are you hungry?" "I heard a noise. Can you come over here and tell me what it is?"

I shared a wall with Wyatt and his long-suffering wife, Marigold. They were not a fun hang. Wyatt was a sensitive songwriter but that's where his sensitivities ended. He talked about himself a lot and I would catch Marigold wincing sometimes as she listened. She did a lot of listening and wore housedresses but in a fashionista way. She was white but wore headwraps. I kept listening at the wall for abuse. I was sure she was going to need my help but she never let on that he was abusive. I listened at the walls for any sign of distress. I wanted to catch him in the act and then be the one to send him to the clink. *I'll get you. I got LAPD on speed dial.*

I didn't really—I hate the cops.

With my new life in the duplex, I decided to get a sports car, you know, to fit into the neighborhood. I was working somewhat steadily and was only responsible for myself. Getting the car was a fairy tale. I traded my gray 1990 Volvo with 182,000 miles on it for this hot rod convertible Mercedes. I got two hundred dollars for the Volvo, but I like to think that the two hundred bucks was for the two milk carton crates full of journals and notes I accidentally left in the trunk. Finally, I got a paycheck for my ideas!

The woman who sold me the exorbitantly priced black Mercedes hard-top convertible was a butch lesbian with dyed blonde hair that flipped over in a swoop to one side like a young Leonardo DiCaprio. She sure saw a mark in me that day. Ace Ventura pet detective sidled right up to me with a grin and a Hawaiian shirt to close the deal. She smiled seductively, "Only five thousand down and a four-year lease . . ."

"That's it?"

"Yep."

"I'm in." I wanted to convince her that I was a baller. *Hell yeah, I'll pay full price no questions asked and five thousand down. Yes, five thousand, I'd pay more!* She wasn't going to get in the way of the sexual chemistry between me and my car. The Grinch stood atop her mountain, wringing her hands, smiling and waving goodbye as I drove into downtown Whoville. I did it!

I named my new car Maurice. He was fast and powerful but so small I could park anywhere! Also, Maurice was magical. Every time I drove home buzzed from the bar, I always seemed to find one spot left to tuck him into around two A.M. Then in the morning, I noticed that Maurice was actually parked not in front of my apartment but a stranger's driveway. No wonder that spot was free! I may have blocked the driveway, but at least I didn't have to take the time to look any longer while drunk, and I did an excellent job parallel parking! I only made this mistake up to four more times, and was forced to correct my behavior when the car got towed. When you live fast and ride hard, this kind of stuff comes with the territory. Going out to the bar every night was my way of not dealing with the pain of my breakup. My self-worth was propped up inside the relationship. Since that had been dismantled, my self-worth was just blowing in the wind. Unfortunately, when you're down like that, you do things like drive drunk and think that it's funny.

At the beginning of our relationship, I had won. We were the it couple. We made out in a dark corner of the bar—hidden, but somehow still in plain sight for all to see. But we were also humble, generous, and soft-spoken, as long as you adhered to the social hierarchy. We were praised and well respected. I was the winner in the competition of getting this creative genius to fall in love with me, thus solidifying that I was also a creative genius. We were the cornerstone of our own social scene.

But without him, I was nothing. I was only an actress. He was a painter who understood the mysteries of art.

The nights where I wasn't out all night getting wasted, I found myself home at the duplex, watching psychic John Edward read people in his studio audience. That gave me comfort. I secretly cried along with the people who recognized their loved ones speaking to them from beyond. That's all I ever wanted, to be validated from the beyond, but it never happened. I could only be validated in the material world through men and now my car, my duplex, and my barfly lifestyle.

Nights that I was home on the early side would be followed by brunch with friends the next day. After mimosas, maybe I'd call José to see if he'd hang out with me or at the very least if he had some dirt on Marigold and Wyatt. He never would. My new hang was with my comedy friends, the ones who understood the depth of my pain and the necessity of day drinking.

My friend Lori turned me on to a restaurant called Shangri-La. We would make a plan to go there and call one of our friends to let them know brunch was on. Then they would tell people and next thing you know ten people were there. I loved being part of a social scene, I hadn't ever experienced that. The outside of the place was painted pink and the metal bars over the doors and windows were painted bright green. This is the first place I ate plantains, black beans, and rice (we didn't have them in Michigan). The inside had a cement floor, the tablecloths were made out of colorful wax paper, and there was religious folk art with Jesus, bleeding hearts, and stars everywhere.

This was the day I sat across from Carlo. He was the Frank Zappa of the comedy scene, the outlier, writing for TV with his friends. He was the white guy who challenged the other white guys in the writers' room. The fact he was interested in me was something I needed. I could only dream of being like him. At the time, I had not yet put together that he was already part of a system that supported him, so he could rebel within the system.

He loved to hang out. It really made me laugh when he begrudgingly ordered himself whiskey for breakfast, as if someone was making him do it. He made it seem like it was part of his life philosophy to "let go" of the traditional expectations of normal and be in the moment. I thought I could learn something from his attitude. It excited me. He was also pro-drug but not in an aggressive way, like my ex-boyfriend. Turns out to hang out with him and learn his lifestyle, all I had to do was show up at the bar he was at. Sitting at bars was his primary activity. He would get sensitive guys together to talk about their dads, or women, or their sexuality over beer. He loved to talk about his own deviant behavior. He had a strict no strings attached policy, which was perfect for me because I was still nursing my breakup. He hung out with a mutual friend of ours, Jim, who I only knew a little bit. I started hanging out with them all the time. Jim was sober, so at the beginning, he drank coffee and smoked cigarettes.

One day, Carlo and Jim picked me up in a beat-up pickup truck to go day drinking. A few months into us all hanging out, I showed up at our favorite bar while Jim and Carlo were in the middle of a discussion about acid. They were planning to do it and seemed really excited about it. "You're going to do acid?" I asked Jim.

"I'm thinking about it. It's time for me to experiment, and I think acid is the way to go." I steered clear from acid because one time I did a little by accident and my mind separated. I was too afraid that it wouldn't come back if I did a full dose. The potential enjoyment factor couldn't outweigh my fear and dislike of the experiences I had already had with psychedelics. That day was the last time I saw Jim sober. He and Carlo were my gateway into my own drug use and an experimental time where I stared at the edge of my own depravity. I was ashamed of my failed relationships and how much I counted on them to be fulfilling. I needed to explore myself, but instead of taking time alone and being with my thoughts and examining my habits, I clouded my mind, body, and emotions in crowded bars with drugs and alcohol. It was a lot of fun. Of course, I ended up dating Jim and doing cocaine with him. He was so much fun, but once the coke was introduced it became about being high in different places. Eventually I made myself stop doing that and our relationship fizzled. That's when I started dating Carlo.

Carlo made me jealous by asking to hang out and then when I arrived at the club, he'd been there talking to three other women. He would frequent strip clubs in LA and took me with him. I wasn't ever in danger, but he made no promises to keep me safe. I thought I was exploring my own sexuality but it was really about him. Me doing what he wanted so that he would want me. Once again, I was codependent with the guy I was into, living my life for him and through him. I tried really hard to not want a relationship with him, but I wasn't the non-monogamous type. He remained committed to not committing. I painted the walls in the bathroom of my cute duplex bright red so I could live in my anger.

One night, Carlo and I made a plan to meet at a bar. It was the beginning of the night and he was sober. I was sober and excited to see him. We both ordered one drink. I sipped mine slowly, like a normal person, excited to be there with him. He panicked at the idea of having a sober one-on-one conversation, so he refused to speak until he quickly downed his first drink (which was already a double) and then got most of the way through his second double. He needed to disappear before he could be with me. Things were somehow serious enough between us and he did believe in genuine heartfelt interaction, so he agreed to go to my therapist with me to try to iron out where our relationship stood.

The week we went, he had pared down his drinking to wine only. This is how he convinced himself he wasn't an alcoholic: "I'll slow down for a while." When I brought up his drinking in therapy, he told my therapist that he was only drinking red wine at meals. He was so charming and sounded so reasonable, she sided with him. What a couple of assholes. In that moment, I lost a boyfriend and a therapist.

When I broke up with Carlo, he promised to get serious. He said he'd do anything to get me back. Any argument he made just seemed even more pathetic because up until that point he acted like he could take it or leave it with me. Suddenly Mr. Cosmic Vibes Whatever guy was a big baby who wasn't getting what he wanted. Now he was leaving long texts about how sorry he was, how much he loved me, and how wrong he had been.

He would beg to see me again, just to talk. When I relented, we talked in an alley and I saw a dead rat. I took it as a sign not to believe him and to move forward. It was time for me to hang up my drinking and drugging lifestyle. I let him sublet my duplex and I gave him money because he was in between jobs and depressed.

I decided to move back to West Hollywood and join Crunch gym. Life was moving ahead. My former neighbor Wyatt was making an independent movie about his life as a musician. Marigold wasn't represented in the script at all; he depicted himself as a genius loner renegade. My agent called me and told me he wanted to offer me a bit part as a grizzled journalist who gives Wyatt a bad review. I turned him down. Luckily, my work was increasing, which really helped me to change my focus from drunken codependent bruncher to full-time professional actress. I was becoming a recognizable character on the TV show *24*, so my life was changing quickly. I remember Carlo visiting me in my trailer one day and his grungy energy was not fitting in with my work vibe. He looked out of place sitting on the bench inside my trailer. His philosophy seemed small now. His demeanor was all about screwing the man and not being mainstream, and here I was being creatively successful and making money.

The only thing he could think to do was make fun of my socks. My character, Chloe, wore thin black footie socks under her work loafers. "Look at your socks. Oh, Chloe!" he said and laughed. It was in that moment I saw his laughter and humor for what it was, a way to cut down the world around him to make himself feel better. Suddenly his counterculture Frank Zappa impersonation was sad. Making fun of my socks was designed to make me feel like the situation was lame, which it was not. I was on a successful TV show as an actress and he couldn't relate, so he tried to belittle my position. Maybe I was supposed to say, "I know my socks are ridiculous," and then I would be down where he was, safe in a place of fear of and mocking what you don't have, acting as if you're better than. If we were in a bar, or at a strip club, it would all be on his terms and I'd have to follow his lead because those were situations I knew less about. But now that he was on my turf, it was clear who the bigger man was, and it wasn't him. I wanted him out of my trailer, which made me feel bad—guilty. That's the part I regret, not the things I did or all the time wasted in bars but the feeling bad or like I owe anyone anything. That's the part I can do without. My job was important to me and I was beginning to have self-respect and my own identity as a working actor. It was time to let go of things that didn't suit me. Goodbye Carlo, hello tiny socks.

# GARRY SHANDLING, ACTING COACH

I had been in Los Angeles going on three years when I was cast to replace Janeane Garofalo on *The Larry Sanders Show*. It's a brilliant show created by Garry Shandling. This show was about Larry Sanders, a late-night talk show host like Jay Leno. It's a meta depiction behind the scenes of the show being made within the show. Janeane played the talent booker. Her career was taking off and she decided to leave the show.

I had done a few guest spots on sitcoms such as *NewsRadio* (as a server at a pirate-themed restaurant) and *Over the Top* with Annie Potts and Tim Curry. I had also been in a few music videos like "The Good Life" by Weezer (as a pizza delivery girl) and "The New Pollution" by Beck (as a girl who cries after pouring a glass of milk). I was also a cast member on *Mr. Show* and had done a lot of live performance. I also did a stand-up set on a show hosted by Janeane Garofalo called *Comedy Product*. My stand-up was still very performance art–heavy. This was where I was mentally at the time. All I wanted to do was perform, but I didn't have the capacity to speak my mind or write clearly. It was working for me. In fact, I was in character as a performance artist. As part of my set I said, "This piece started five minutes ago when I took ecstasy." I hadn't really taken ecstasy. It was a comedic device to give the audience permission to laugh at the non sequiturs I was spewing. I showed drawings of different combs on notebook paper and attempted to explain my artistic vision but I kept getting distracted because I was "on drugs." This was the tape that my manager submitted to casting.

That got me a meeting with Garry Shandling and his head writer John Riggi. I was seated in a director's chair opposite John and Garry. Garry said something to the effect of "So how's it going?"

I shot back, "Great. How's it going with you?" There was no material for me to read. And I had no idea how to act in a meeting so I just stared. Then, Garry said, "What brings you here today?" I said, "I have no idea." He replied, "That's what I thought." He stared at me for an awkward beat and then started to laugh. That made me laugh. Life was ridiculous and we all knew it. They whispered to each other and then the meeting was over. I got the part. I was very fortunate to get the part this way. These were two creators who were confident in their vision and knew what they wanted after getting a feel for a person in the room. That person was me and my character's name was Mary Lou.

One day, a few episodes in, Mary Lou was going to get a cup of coffee in the bullpen. She runs into Larry Sanders, who asks "How's it going?" but really he's worried about something that's going on with a guest on the show and the booking. I know information but I don't want to let on to him that I know. At the time, when I was acting I wasn't thinking about intention or choices. I was simply delivering the words.

Garry called me out. He asked that the cameras stop rolling. He stared at me. "Why are you saying what you're saying?" I laughed uncomfortably. He followed that up with "What is your character thinking about right now? What does she really mean when she says that?" I stared at him. Then he became stern. He asked again and indicated that my character might feel one way or the other about what she was saying. The cameras weren't rolling and he was giving me a crash course acting lesson right then and there. He was disappointed that I hadn't given it any thought, but he still took the time to show me the way. He waited until he saw I had gotten the idea and we moved forward. Luckily, I was a quick study and after that day, I never went to the set without knowing my character's intention again. I am forever grateful to be able to have learned on the job and for the chance he took by hiring me.

# TOM CRUISE

There's an immediate closeness between actors and their hair and makeup team. The relationship is collaborative and intimate. They create your look for the movie and in turn you showcase their talent and vision. Usually, they are kind, sensitive, and supportive. They are the most fun to go to parties and gossip with. Once during lunch on an independent movie, my makeup artist, Cori, and I hopped on electric scooters and rode to get pictures of our auras taken. Ninety-five percent of the time, the hair and makeup team is your ally. The other 5 percent of the time they are mean. This was the case when I worked on the film *Magnolia*. And remember, these were the people who were the gateway to me being styled for a scene where I'm on a date with *Tom Cruise*.

In *Magnolia*, Tom Cruise's character is a motivational speaker giving a seminar about how to influence people and win over women. During his speech, he gives an example of how you manipulate women. My character, Janet, his young assistant, was the woman he was thinking of, so it cuts to the scene with me.

I went for my second costume fitting after the holiday break and someone I didn't know in the costume department walked by me and said, "Oh, someone ate a lot during Christmas." No one had ever talked to me like that. It wasn't something that I thought about, but now he had planted the seed. *Should I be worried about my weight? Will I be able to fit into my wardrobe? Will Tom Cruise refuse to be in the scene with me?* It really affected my self-esteem. Especially because it was coming from someone I was looking to be validated by. Someone who was literally putting the clothes on my back.

That first moment I saw Tom Cruise was shortly before our scene. People flocked around him like moths to a flame. They couldn't help it. Even people who were not normally starstruck were drawn to him. There was a magnetic pull going out fifty feet all around him. I imagine it was like this wherever he went. And he was so friendly, you felt like he wanted to talk to you. But you never actually felt close to him. I knew I wouldn't be around him again, but I had my moment of grace. I told him about my new stick-shift car. I had gotten a 1989 Volkswagen Rabbit. It had windows that needed to be physically rolled down. I remember driving to set and it was raining, the stick shift wasn't fully working, and the windows fogged up and never unfogged. So trying to drive it there was scary. I couldn't see the road. Also, it was manual. I told him how I got that car and it was scary to try to shift in the rain, and he said, "Yeah, stick shifts can be really fun!" *Fun works differently when you're Tom Cruise.*

In the scene we were about to shoot, his character, TJ Mackey, was late coming to my character, Janet's, house for a date. During our scene, his character was upset and he wanted to be crying real tears at the same point in the scene for each take. He did a very professional actor thing where if he couldn't get the tears the way he wanted he would say, "Hold the roll!" and walk off set into a private area. He would do some secret magic with his own emotions and then you'd hear in full Tom Cruise hero voice, "OK, I'm ready," as he marched back on set, and that would be the cue for the cameras to start rolling and he'd walk right into the scene with tears rolling down his cheeks. He wasn't afraid to see himself cry. It was powerful.

One time on *24*, there was a very quick one-shot scene of me sobbing in a bathroom stall. The crew was all business moving equipment, getting sandwiches, yakking it up. They had me stand in for myself while they quickly lit the bathroom. I didn't have any spare seconds to do my actor magic on my emotions. "OK let's go!" the assistant director yelled. No one asked if I was ready. I guess we were filming! I pretended the toilet was my scene partner.

Since it was such a quick moment, the crew was already onto the next shot in their minds. The problem was that I needed to sob. I might as well have been the bathroom door as far as they were concerned. "The actor isn't instantly sobbing. Let's take some screws out, move it, and get a different angle." I was able to work up a couple of tears and let my face and voice do the rest of the sobbing. The trick is to imagine something terrible happening to someone you love. Did I ruin acting for you?

I didn't have the balls to yell "Hold the roll," like Tom Cruise. What if I did and then it wasn't worth it? I'd leave the set to go into a private corner and march back in, all Maverick-style, announcing, "I'm ready!" Everyone would be staring at me, thinking, *What did we wait for? This performance?!* Better to just blend in with the bathroom door. But like a human door that is crying. That would be easier.

In TJ Mackey's speech, he talks about how to manipulate women. Then you see my character, Janet, at my apartment, pissed off that he's late. He arrives on the doorstep, crying. TJ Mackey tells his audience that all you have to do to win a woman over is be emotional and lie. He tells me a story about how he saved some puppies or how he hit a puppy and had to take it to the hospital. I warm up to him because you know how bitches are and then next thing you know, we're on the couch, making out! Did I forget to mention that it was a make-out scene?! He feels up my breast over my shirt during the kissing. After each take, I jumped up off the couch and burst into laughter. (That's the same way I was on *24*, in a scene where I was being tortured. The second it was over, they would say "cut" and I would be laughing and making jokes because I was so embarrassed about acting.)

Anyway, my make-out scene with Tom Cruise in *Magnolia* ended up on the cutting-room floor. The scene took place inside his character's mind, and there were so many other storylines that it didn't make the cut. I do have another scene where he's in a stairwell yelling at me on the phone and you hear my voice. I like to think that the world wasn't ready for my make-out scene with Tom Cruise. But maybe it's because I was too fat. (It definitely wasn't that, but now I'll always have this thought attached to this moviemaking experience, so thanks for that, loathsome costumer.) I guess we'll never know. I'll settle for my voice being in the movie. That was the first time I made out with Tom Cruise. Also, it was the last time.

# YES, AND

One of the most popular questions I get asked by *24* fans is: "What was it like being Kiefer Sutherland's sidekick?" It is hard for some *24* loyalists to understand that in real life we were not a team saving the country but instead coworkers filming a show together.

One morning a few seasons into the show, I drove across town to the local Fox television affiliate studio to do press interviews. It was three thirty A.M. I needed to get dressed and have my hair and makeup done by five A.M. to sit in a chair with an earpiece and stare at a blank screen but act as if I were talking directly to the voices that were in my ear. I was gearing up to be interviewed back-to-back by morning news anchors from different syndicates in different cities across the country. First comes the technical director to let me know who is coming on and which city is next. There are around twenty-five stations from all over the country that were timed for five-minute segments, one after the other. Usually, two hosts will hop into my ear and say how excited they are for the next season of *24*. I'd hint at storylines but wouldn't say too much. I'd smile and laugh and say how happy I am to be here and how excited I am about the show. But on this particular morning, the questions that were asked of me were very different. Right out of the gate, Heather Burkowitz from San Antonio (fake name and city) said, "Good morning Mary Lynn, it's so nice to see you! So, as Kiefer's girl Friday Chloe O'Brian, on Fox's hit television show *24*, you always have Jack's back. Would you have his back in a bar fight?"

"What?"

"That happened last night in Manhattan! You know Kiefer. Do you think he was defending a woman's honor?"

I knew that to me this behavior was childish, ridiculous, and dangerous but he was also my boss. I didn't want to make waves.

They just wanted something to chew up and spit out and I wasn't going to give it to them. Whatever transgressions he allegedly committed are his business.

Also, honestly, I was intimidated by him in real life. I was also worried that if I tried to speak to him, I would screw up and I really wanted to keep my job. So, I tried to not be around him as much as I could. There would be fewer opportunities for me to screw up.

"I'm sure that's what he was doing. He definitely fights for what is right on-screen and off." Every interview revolved around his alleged head-butting episode from the night before. At the time, I thought I had no choice but to "have his back" for a situation that I knew nothing about and didn't want to discuss.

I saw the headline later: "Kiefer Sutherland Head Butts Designer Defending Brooke Shields, Shields Denies."

The article reported that the man was friends with Brooke and that Kiefer was intoxicated. The designer was quoted as saying, "He was drunk, wouldn't back down or be logical, and pulled some frat boy wrestling move like a teenager." I didn't get this information until after my whirlwind press junket with the affiliates via satellite was over.

It was part of the exchange for being on the show—you had to put up with some unorthodox uncomfortable things—but I believed it was part of my job to represent the show and him and paint it all in a good light. And as Kiefer's fictional sidekick, that's what I did.

# MARK OF A STARLET

I was invited to the Monte-Carlo Television Festival, an event I had never heard of. Monte Carlo is the place where all the men are in tuxedos, smoking thin cigarettes, and the ladies are in long, flowing gowns, dripping in diamonds. The place where James Bond pulled out his pistol in *Casino Royale*. The Principality of Monaco had requested my presence! The festival couldn't get Kiefer Sutherland to go so they asked me, Dennis Haysbert, who played President David Palmer, and our executive producer, Jon Cassar. The three of us would surely equal the star power of Kiefer! Although they have been doing the festival for the past sixty years, no one knows this is a thing.

I felt fantastic about receiving an all-expenses-paid trip, borrowing dresses and a ten-thousand-dollar tennis bracelet. This seemed like the least I could do. The trip was exhausting, but when you fly first-class and get champagne and you know there is no obligation other than to just show up dressed up and stay standing upright, what is there to be worried about? It was like being in a dream. But not a dream you worked your whole life for, a dream that just happened to you—something I was picked up and plopped into like a cake topper shoved into the frosting of a super-sweet three-layer cake. Would I be able to eat through to the bottom of the cake and land on the plate? No, I was to sit atop and look around at the world whilst the cake was being displayed before being eaten by others.

I had a hotel room above the Casino de Monte-Carlo. I woke up to my non-English-speaking hair and makeup team. "What do you think of this dress?" Does this work?" I asked, modeling my white BCBG lace sundress. They said, *"Oui,"* as I bit into another croissant, each new croissant was the best croissant I had ever eaten in my life. It was served with butter and jam. I sipped cappuccino and sat down to let them get to work on my face and hair.

I slipped into my white day-into-night, mid-length strapless dress and high-heeled sandals and pulled out the jewelry I had borrowed for the trip. It was a tennis bracelet, a ring, and chandelier earrings. I had kept the jewelry on my person for the entire trip, not wearing it but clutching it close to my body. Not leaving it out of my sight.

When I cascaded downstairs and out the door of the hotel, a small throng of fans descended on me. My French-speaking handler, who was assigned to make sure I got to where I was going, stepped aside so I could greet them. They all spoke in French and swarmed me. When this happened in the United States, I always had a publicist lightly put their hand on my back and guide me as they told the fans, "She has to keep moving, she's late!" Or if it was a really big event, they would line up the fans behind a barrier so they could see me and say hi but not move closer.

This kind of thing came with the territory when you were on one of the top-five TV shows on the air for five years running. There were also a few times a couple of "fans" would be waiting at the airport with a stack of photos, trying to trick me into signing as many as possible so they could sell them on the internet. Just like that, something about this felt off. They had an exceptionally hyper energy and no photos to sign. I remember thinking, *Do they even know the show? Why do they want my attention?* No one yelled my name or Kiefer's. In fact, a few of them looked disheveled. I felt bad for them. If this was really exciting for them and they came here to catch a glimpse of me, the least I could do was stop. I didn't know what the etiquette was, and since I was a guest in this country, I thought, *I don't want to be rude or do the wrong thing.* I didn't want to insult them—maybe that's how the fans were here. I had no idea.

One woman had a random scrap of paper for me to sign. She had a forlorn angry look in her eyes. I wanted to act appropriately, so I stopped and signed autographs. Then they disappeared as quickly as they had arrived. I knew in my gut that something was off with this huddle of greasy people trying to get my attention. It wasn't until later that I figured out what.

After a couple of interviews, we were taken to the palace of the Prince of Monaco. We drove through very narrow streets like in a *Mission Impossible* car chase. We drove down one such corridor, until it got so narrow that our car could no longer fit through so we reversed out of there and took another tiny, brick-walled street. When we arrived at the palace, we were dropped off at a large courtyard. It was more yard than court. It was large and all dark gray cobblestones from the thirteenth century. I remember milling about and being told how to act when the prince arrives.

We were not to touch him, but we could say hello and do a slight bow. It would have been fantastic to get a historical tour; instead, we got a champagne brunch with a huge group of celebrities. The only ones I recognized were Lauren Holly, Hugh Hefner, and his three girlfriends, who had a show at the time called *The Girls Next Door*. It was Holly Madison, Kendra, and the other one. Ironically, I felt the most comfortable chatting with Kendra. She was the most relatable person in the whole place.

"We're totally partying at the prince's castle," I said.

"We're totally at the prince's castle!" she repeated, mocking me in a robotic voice. I repeated it again back to her while doing a robot dance to make her laugh. After a few minutes and a photo op, Kendra and I parted ways. I stood looking over a balcony, awkwardly alone, wondering where my friends were, and when I turned to walk back through the palace to mingle, I noticed that my borrowed tennis bracelet was not on my wrist. I panicked and instantly put my head down and began scouring the floor. I traced my steps backward, which was strange because no one but security guards were back near the front door. The party had started outside, circulated through part of the palace, and was nearing the final room before we would exit. People were casually lining up to say goodbye to the prince in the same type of receiving line as we had said hello.

I found Jon Cassar, his wife, Dennis Haysbert, and his manager at the bar, grabbing a final cocktail and whispered that I had somehow lost my bracelet. Everyone started looking. Even Lauren Holly. We all gave it a good try and finally gave up. I was beside myself; everyone offered up a few minutes of concern and advice and then went on with their evening. I felt sick.

My publicist broke the news to the place that had lent it to me and it was out of my hands. I felt bad but I really didn't have to deal with the loss or breaking the news at all. It would be covered by insurance. That would be the last time I borrowed expensive jewelry.

On the plane back, I was falling asleep and those fans outside the hotel popped into my head. I bolted awake. They took my bracelet! I will never be able to prove it. But it's the only thing that makes sense. *The bracelet wouldn't fall off. And they didn't really have any interest in me. It was more chaos and . . . distraction!* I was their mark and they got a diamond bracelet for their day's work. How could I think they were so feverishly there for me, not knowing my name, my character's name, or even the name of the show I was on? I got duped. If I ever see Kendra again, I bet she would agree. I would say to her in a robot voice, "They stole my bracelet, right?" They saw a gullible American with no idea how pickpocketing works. It felt like more of an embarrassment than a violation. I felt dumb that they were able to get away with it. Sometimes when you're faking it and trying to do the right thing, you actually just make yourself an easy mark. I learned my lesson in Monte Carlo. And I still don't understand what a principality is.

# MY WOMEN'S COMMUNE

It was the mid-2000s, and I was with a guy named Sean. He was very childlike. He told me how much he loved me and how beautiful I was. We used to drink together. And frolic. He was the first guy I dated in Los Angeles who was an artist type and believed in God. It was refreshing. He talked to me about me instead of talking about himself. It was a relief to be around him. He was really into drugs and aliens and was a practicing Latter-day Saint. He smiled a lot and was joyful. Sean turned me on to Christian music and a lot of stories about the end of times. It was really sweet.

We lived together in a bungalow in Venice that I paid for with the money I made from films like *Julie & Julia* and *Little Miss Sunshine*. It was a happy time. Sean and I had a modern relationship where the roles of man and woman weren't so rigidly defined. I would go to work on the set, and he would stay home to cook and make sculpture. It seemed like the perfect situation. He asked me to marry him and I said yes. One day while I was making invitations and he was making a nude statue out of cardboard boxes, coffee grounds, and our AT&T bill, I took a break and went to Bristol Farms gourmet food mart, where I ran into an old friend of mine named Barb.

Barb was a woman I dated in my late twenties around 1995. We had dated when we were both servers at Buca de Beppa, an Italian restaurant in the San Fernando Valley. Take a minute with that.

We had a passionate relationship. I left her because she was very demanding, jealous, and emotional. I'll never forget when she called me twelve times in a row and I didn't answer. When I called her back, she didn't answer. I went to her place and found her sitting on the kitchen floor drawing on herself with a Sharpie. That was when I decided this might not be a good person to date.

Now, ten years later, here we were at a fancy grocery store, I was buying Greek yogurt and she was buying a rotisserie BBQ chicken. We had both grown up so much. We were both amazing! She was now a real estate and money mogul because she listened to Suze Orman and read a book called *Rich Dad Poor Dad*. I was also a big deal, having become an international superstar since the last time she saw me. I'm humble, so I wasn't acting like I was a big deal but she knew it. It was really nice to see her. We got a crew together and started to hang out again. Barb, her girlfriend, Sean, and myself. My life was really coming together—it was really nice to be with a guy who was so sweet and hang out with our friends.

It was around this time that my beach bungalow was broken into. I was so angry with myself for leaving the window open. I felt violated but also like it was meant to happen. That's what I deserved for leaving the window open and the bike outside, and my laptop on the table. I filed a police report. Sean wasn't sure how to act. He said he was vulnerable and wanted to have sex. So we made love. Then he wrote a poem from the thief's perspective.

When I mentioned to Barb what had happened, she came right away to assess the situation. She insisted I buy an alarm system. She made an appointment for me to meet with the alarm company, which was such a caring thing for a friend to do. I admired her willingness to take charge and go above and beyond. But I don't believe in alarms. This was a petty crime that was the result of me not locking the window. Having an alarm system was not necessary, but I went along with it anyway because Barb was so adamant. I signed a year-long contract. The alarm was high tech: It was laser beams in front of all the doors and windows. If a beam was disturbed, the company would immediately send out a car with an armed guard. I set off the alarm six times in the first week, the annoyance of which was compounded by the fact that I never remembered the password to reset it. Eventually, I just stopped setting the alarm and continued to pay for it.

Shortly after, Sean and I started having problems, and I realized that it takes more than someone idolizing you and not buying Starbucks to make a relationship work. They have to have a job beyond making sculptures out of trash.

"I think you need to go get your life together."

"What do you mean? Aren't you set for life?"

"Move out please. Maybe we can get back together when you learn how to take care of yourself."

"Can I get the ring and the mattress?"

Sean and I didn't make it down the aisle. Now I was alone in the romantic beach bungalow. Luckily I still had Barb and her girlfriend, Jen. Their other friend Rebecca was going through a divorce. When we hung out, you could feel the girl power. We commiserated and drank red wine, and I learned that Barb was having problems with Jen! I couldn't believe it—they had been together for years. I was counting on them to be my lesbian rock. Barb started to talk about Jen with such disdain. She said she needed to break up with her. Barb and Rebecca and I would spend nights processing what went wrong and what all of our next moves would be.

We started to make jokes about starting a women's commune. One day I thought, *Why not.* Why not move in with my new best friends. Rebecca needed a place and Barb was a genius about investments. She said I absolutely could afford a two-million-dollar house. We decided to follow this dream of me buying a house for all of us by emptying my bank account. That will show the patriarchy!

The house was in Woodland Hills, California. It had a saltwater pool with iridescent blue Italian tiles. There was a tennis court, an aviary—which was a completely fenced-in outside area covered with the largest tarp I've ever seen (apparently the birds were under the tarp)—and a guesthouse. It had a steam shower connected to the side of the bathroom with a tiled mosaic in it, of a woman pouring water out of a jug. The fixtures were brass. I began the process of buying the house but didn't have enough for the down payment. Barb convinced me to borrow over one hundred grand from Rebecca's soon-to-be ex until my paychecks came in to cover the cost. What a great idea! A soon-to-be ex who was a man. So yeah, fuck men. Who do they think they are? Trusting you to repay them one hundred thousand dollars. I felt odd pre-spending a bunch of my TV paychecks but everyone else was OK with it. But mostly Barb. She thought this was a great idea—and we had to act fast if we wanted to get the house. You know, the biggest purchase of your life that puts you in debt for thirty years, gotta hurry! When we moved in, we were told that the birds were still under the tarp and that the previous owner would come back for them. Those birds didn't make a peep, and then one day, the tarp was gone and the cage was empty. It was very mysterious.

Barb was so thoughtful and caring that right before she moved in, she got a rescue dog. Not just any rescue dog. One from Florida without a butthole. An anus-less dog from Pensacola. She flew to get the dog, brought him back, and paid for his surgery to get an anus put in. So then I bought the house with my TV money and she moved that bleeding-anus-bulldog in there. Rebecca moved in with her daughter Pinky, who wanted to paint her bedroom Pink. They brought a male pug named Marky, who wanted to mark every room. I fucking hate pugs and children to this day. To people who say that pugs or kids are so cute I say, "Fuck off!" Why I had more tolerance for the bleeding anus is obvious. That pug was peeing on things out of spite. He was jealous of my TV money.

Unfortunately, there were plenty of rooms to pee in. The house was six thousand square feet. It was built around a court-yard in back with French doors from all the bedrooms that led onto the patio. All the floors were granite. Lots of wrought iron. In the kitchen there was a bread-warming drawer, a built-in wok, a temperature-controlled wine cellar, and everything a chef who would never live there would need.

We went to Bed Bath & Beyond and bought towels together. We got toilet paper to spare for the six bathrooms and had wine-tasting parties. This was our new lifestyle. One night we had a book-burning party for fun. We were censoring our own lives, burning what felt harmful to us. Burning ideas to set us free and brazenly destroy-ing our former culture to create our own culture. Our new culture included not really being clear about our expectations, desires, and boundaries. We just moved in like roommates in a dorm. The college was a mansion I paid for and the only person learning a lesson was me. Barb and Rebecca did buy towels and a coffeemaker, but they did not pay rent of any kind. Is that how communes work?

On the surface it was fun. I loved having a mansion. The vast amount of space gave me an air of success. On the other hand, when it wasn't exuding success, it was creating enormous pressure to clean, decorate, and maintain. Thinking, *I'm a big shot! This is so fun to celebrate my success with all of you!* quickly became, *I'm hemorrhaging money on this house that has never-ending expenses, living with people under no obligation to share the burden, and with whom I have no lasting bond.*

And yet somehow I continued to bestow authority on Barb. She would tell me, matter-of-factly, what to spend money on. One day I came home and there were roofers.

"Javier says it's going to cost thirty thousand to replace this."

"Are you serious?"

"Yes, I'm afraid the roof needs to be done now."

"Whatever you say."

She was the expert, she would take care of it. She and Javier would have no problem spending my thirty grand. I gave her dominion over my finances. I found out that her real talent with finances seemed to be spending other people's money. I don't think she had any money in her bank account. She just had a lot of ideas about money. I would keep my head in the clouds, work my dream job, and go with the flow.

What were we to each other? A witches' coven? Were they my wives? My philosophy of life was to let people in my life if they approached me. If they were opinionated and gave me attention, I would begin to react to their wants and needs and try to become what they wanted and needed. But just enough to get by and without investigating my own wants and needs.

I had agreed to be Barb's life partner but I didn't really mean it. I knew she wanted to be with me and she had convinced me that she was the only one in the world I could really trust. I thought we were real estate moguls together and now we shared the same physical space. My feeling was that Barb thought I was delicate, artistic, and in need of a strong hand to guide me. I, in turn, believed she was so emotionally fucked up that if I let her think she was fixing me, that would fix her. I promised her a shared space and then avoided figuring out the specifics. She took that to mean no boundaries. Being in the house with all these women was forcing me to figure out my boundaries through trial by fire.

One morning Barb got up at four thirty to make me a smoothie because my call time for work was five A.M. Nothing like being forced to act grateful for something you're not expecting and don't want. I hate smoothies and I hate being up in the morning before dawn. Now you gotta make me act, before I even get to work for an *actual* acting job. Another time, I was sick in bed with a sinus infection and just wanted to rest. She came to the bedside giving me pain relievers and Vicks VapoRub, and attempted to put a Breathe Right strip over the bridge of my nose. "Jesus Christ! Stop touching my nose!" I pushed her away.

"You don't want to be taken care of? Fine!" She threw the Tylenol across the room.

*How are you angry at me and why? Because I'm sick?* I didn't say that at the time. I thought it. It occurred to me we had agreed to be life partners because she wanted to be my life partner, but we weren't having sex and now we weren't even getting along. We were sleeping in the same bed and still not having sex. It was a massive Cal King bed in which every night we rolled over to our sides, a world away. Me with zero desire to be near her let alone have sex with her. I would try to have the bare minimum of conversation with her before traveling to my continent of the bed.

"Toby's butthole seems to be healing."

"Yeah, there's a lot less leaking."

"I'm so proud of him."

"Me too."

"Good night."

"Good night."

We did this for months. Then one day I mustered up the courage to say, "Barb, we're not having sex. That's not a good sign."

She said, "I know. That's OK. I'll wait."

"Wait for what?" I meant to say, *I am repulsed by you. I hate you. You are controlling and emotionally withholding. You scare and shame me into being with you. You act like you want to be close to me but you lie to yourself.*

I would lie there fantasizing about being in the bed alone and developed insomnia so I would get up in the middle of the night and walk around the block. One night I dreamt that I was in prison with my sister. My sister went to the corner of our cell where there was a small window to the outside world. The sun was coming in. There were thick bars on the window. I yelled, "We're going to get out of this jail!" Then she pulled down a shade that was in front of the bars and it was completely dark.

The next day I told Barb she had to go.

We had a passive-aggressive argument.

"You need me here! You can't do all this without me. I know you're not serious right now," she said. Barb told me I was stingy and selfish—that I was breaking the agreement. She told me she was the only one who could take care of me and that I was too stubborn to see that. I tried to reason with her but she was too strong and too loud. Her anger was rising. We were in the bedroom. The bedroom was the size of most apartments. I wanted to hear her, to reason with her, to listen, to talk it out to get her to see that this was all wrong. A voice inside of me said, *Yell. Yell now. Get her out of the bedroom. Get her out of the house. Yell anything. Don't think about it.*

"You don't know what you're saying or doing! I don't believe you. You are not my keeper! You can't talk to me like that. Bla bla," I yelled and yelled as I walked forward pushing her with my voice and physicality into the backyard.

Yell and walk forward. Yell and walk forward. Push her out of the house. It worked!

I started yelling. "You can't talk to me like that! This isn't working and you need to leave. Also, you're mean!" We stood in the backyard and the wind whipped around us. It was like *The Seventh Seal.* Demonic winds stirred up as she tried to use the dark side to overpower me. The dogs ran in a circle around us, barking. I felt the fury rise and threaten to take me. I kept yelling until finally she walked away to the guesthouse. She took her Harley-Davidson belt buckle and motorcycle boots with her.

I rarely saw Barb after that. She stayed in the guesthouse. There were no more dinners together. Rebecca and I banded together, having clandestine talks about how we were going to get Barb to leave. We came up with nothing. We didn't know how to do it. Luckily, she left about a month later on her own.

Shortly after Barb had been gone a few weeks, Rebecca retreated into her room, taking a coffeemaker in there to minimize having to encounter me. I finally got up the courage to talk to her about what she wanted to do. I gently asked if she wanted to stay and start contributing rent.

"I have tennis elbow. I can't get a job waiting tables."

"Oh I see, that's too bad."

The next week she got a new puppy. She couldn't pay rent or work but she thought it was a good idea to get a puppy.

Eventually, Rebecca moved out and I was in the biggest house all by myself. Strangely, to this day, I don't regret any of it. I could have a nest egg right now if I had spent less and invested like a normal person. I'm glad I got to know what it was like to have a house like that. It was beautiful and stressful and unnecessary.

As far as emotionally abusive relationships go, Barb was a fun one. We even got married at a voodoo ceremony by homeless strangers in New Orleans one time. Breaking up with her and getting back my mansion that I couldn't afford gave me the strength and vision to move forward. I would eventually sell that mansion for way less than I paid for it. It was a foreclosure and my credit was damaged.

Rebecca moved out of state and I'm really not sure if she cured that tennis elbow. Her daughter grew up and got a nose ring. We heard on Facebook (which was new at the time) through a friend of a friend that Barb moved to New Orleans upon leaving my mansion. Within six weeks she was pregnant with the baby of an out-of-work trumpet player that she met on Yahoo personals. All's well that ends well, I suppose.

# MY QUARTERBACK BOYFRIEND

I am a stand-up comic. In 2019, I went on the road, opening for Fred Armisen. We went in a coach bus with a small crew across the country and played in mostly rock venues for audiences of two thousand people. His shows were sold out and the audiences were almost as generous as he was. After each show there would be a meet and greet where about 250 people would wait to tell Fred their favorite thing he's done and for him to know that they are his number-one fan and destined to be friends with him forever. And Fred, being Fred, would speak to each person for two to seven minutes. You do the math. That's a lot of glad-handing for a guy that's not going to be president. I would stand at the other end of his merch and photo table. After the magic of meeting him, they'd meander all pie-eyed up to me: "Hey you've been on a show too!" I was the sloppy-seconds bonus celeb they didn't know was going to be there. "Can I get a picture?!" I'd say, "Of course! This is so fun. I am so humble and just happy to be here hoping you might notice me and want my picture too!" (Guzzle red wine in red Solo cup.)

After the meet and greet, we would pack up and get in the tour van and drive all night. Wheels up would change slightly every night. "Van leaves at two A.M.! We drive eight hours to the next show in Houston." So we would hole up in our sleeping pods until the next morning, arriving dirty, hungry, and foggy from rolling around in the back of the van all night while our trusty driver, Mike, took care of business. Mike really liked us, because unlike his last tour he didn't have to wear a bulletproof vest and carry a gun. Our tiny crew of a tour manager, merch person, two sound people, me, and Fred were quiet. We didn't trash the van with whores and bottles of booze. Only one of us drank heavily in secret. We were all conscious of other people's personal space—"Oops excuse me, sorry"—as inevitably you'd run into someone, since we all shared one bathroom and one walkway. Usually, each person would get up at their own time and wander out into the city, looking for the best nearby coffee. We would have hotel rooms for a few hours during the day to rest, stretch out, and get ready for the show. This was really nice, but it also felt strange to be using the rooms at the opposite hours of everyone else. There was a lot of downtime.

It was also strange to be doing this in my late forties. Acting like a rock star rolling into cities, leaving my pets, my husband, and my kid back home. Who was going to take my position on the hospitality committee at my son's progressive private school while I was gone? It was unusual but it gave me time to contemplate my crumbling marriage in different cities and states. Each vista would find me looking out the window, wondering if we were going to make it.

On the days we had hotel rooms, which were all in a certain high-standard hotel chain, thanks to the generosity of Fred Armisen, during check-in, the employees would always go into their spiel about the hotel and its amenities. It was hard to wait through the speeches about parking and what time the bar closes and towel service and if you want housekeeping at a certain time. *Maybe I could just tell you the two things I do need,* I'd think to myself, *which is a shower and to be in a bed that's not moving and is bigger than a coffin. Don't these hospitality employees understand that not all guests are created equal? I don't need your parking or your gym or your mini bar, I just need to crash for a few hours, man.*

This hotel in Lincoln, Nebraska, was the most obnoxious because it was themed. It was a late-fifties/early-sixties time capsule with modern touches. Lots of plaid. Look at us. We're different! Notice the curtains behind my desk when you're checking in are replicas of the curtains from the Johnny Carson show.

I don't want to be upbeat and excited now. Nostalgia is what got me into my relationship in the first place. I'm a grown woman from Los Angeles, I have a husband and child, and you're shoving your kitsch and craft cocktails down my throat. Why is the front desk girl talking so loudly at me?

"There's virtual golf in the back bar every day during happy hour."

This hotel is very stylish for Lincoln, Nebraska. I hope it single-handedly makes Lincoln a tourist destination. But I don't want any of it right now or maybe ever. It felt like she wished I would compliment her fifties hairstyle. I just don't have that kind of time. All I could think was: *I'm sticky.*

"Furthermore, the pie-eating competition is at noon tomorrow . . ."

"I won't be here tomorrow."

"Would you like to rent a hula hoop or a pogo stick?"

"I just want to change my underwear!"

I made it up to my room, which I soon discovered to be not only fifties themed but "college from the fifties" themed. There was a composition book and sharpened pencils on the desk. Pom-poms in the corner and spirit flags on the wall. Do I have to take a test before I can shower?! I feel like I'm late for class and about to fail the exam. It's my recurring nightmare brought to life.

The room was designed to make you feel nostalgic for, as the triangle banner read in the bathroom, "the best years of your life." I don't care who put the dip dadip dadip in the rama lama lama ding dong so stop asking me! Get off my back! I fell into a fitful, sweaty, rage-filled nap, dreaming that my fifties-style jock boyfriend was beating up every fan in line after Fred's show. He barely broke a sweat in his varsity jacket, pummeling the guy who asked me for a hug. His big, strong knuckle with a class ring punching his nose. "Leave her alone. She's my girl! She's wearing my pin!" I woke up embarrassed and sad.

My best friend growing up, Courtney, broke up with me in the seventh grade so she could place all of her attention on her first boyfriend, quarterback of the JV football team, Bill. She got his class ring and tied blue yarn around it until it fit on her finger. When she wore that and his letter jacket, it was embarrassing. She wore it as a safety blanket and to show off. I thought it was gross but I still wanted it. Really, I just wanted her back. I wanted her to want to be with me more than she did him. I was no longer needed. I kept waiting for her to snap out of it. Instead, she left me forever. We weren't friends past seventh grade.

OK no problem, Courtney. I'll just date one of his friends from the team so we can still hang out and double date! But it turns out, I didn't want to look at let alone talk to any football players. Not one of them knew who David Bowie was. I don't know how she did it.

When I was in my mid-thirties, I had given up on men. All my relationships were with artists. They all love to talk about their feelings. None of them were into sports. But also, none of them could sustain a relationship and neither could I. Then it happened. I saw him as soon as I walked into the Improv comedy club on Melrose, with his baseball cap not completely on his head, staring off, looking dangerous in his low-riding pants. He was the quarterback and the criminal all rolled into one and the most beautiful man I had ever seen. Too young and too good-looking for me. I was flabbergasted when he asked for my number.

He and his friend had chatted me up and Matt, the male model six-foot-two-inch quarterback, barely said five words. His friend did all the talking, but Matt was the one who followed me as I was leaving and asked for my number. That's what he does. He's a closer, you know, he doesn't have to say anything because he looks so good. He's going to come out and get my digits and close the deal. I only said my number once. He was ready to hear those numbers. He remembered that shit and called me.

He left a voicemail. His voice was so sexy on the phone. I called and left him a message: "I'll meet you for one drink. Let's meet at the same place where we met. Same time, same place. Listen, I'll have about thirty minutes before I need to be somewhere else." So that became the unspoken dynamic. I was a woman in charge and he was a young guy who could have anyone and chose to be with me. We played this game of "Am I good enough for you? Are you good enough for me?" Both of our attractions based on our image of what we thought we were and how we wanted the other person to see us. I thought he would leave me for a young model, and he thought I would leave him for an old guy who owned a private jet.

*This is my new thing: I'm going to tell him how it's going to go down and he's going to take care of me and lift things. I'll learn how to throw a ball and catch a ball. I'm going to wear his letter jacket and his class ring. He's going to put his arm around me and I'll be all tiny wrapped in his hug.*

The second time we met, he picked me up and twirled me and I was hooked, no questions asked. I decided I was going to make the image real. A good-looking jock guy and his lady. We dated. I got pregnant and we got married. Now it was ten years later and the marriage was on the rocks.

The kitschy hotel was triggering. I was trying to be away from my problems and here they all were, following me.

I made assumptions that it would work out. That we would grow together. He wasn't who I thought he was and we did not grow together. I tried to give him what he needed, but it wasn't enough and he wasn't enough for me.

Normally, I'd go on the road for a weekend and come back home to my husband asking me how it went because I told him to ask me how it went. There was never a real interest on his part to know who I was or what I had been going through. I made myself OK with that for a decade. I found other people to talk to about being a comic on the road. I talked to friends about struggles and worries. I waited for him to initiate sex with me once in a blue moon. This time, I was on the road, knowing that the ties were being cut. I wasn't willing to be so alone in my marriage anymore. I decided it would be better for us to separate and he didn't argue. I was tired of waiting for him to want to be around me, and I'm guessing he was tired of being pressured to show up.

This tour with Fred felt different—I was constantly reminded that I was about to embark on the rest of my life as a divorced person. I was trying to clear my head, but my head was too full and the nostalgic hotel wasn't helping. I needed neutrals, not plaid pillowcases or virtual golf happy hour. I needed to mourn my marriage.

Maybe it wasn't the hotel's fault. A hotel full of soft beiges I'm sure would have triggered me in another way. Doing shows every night and driving around the country was not a bad way to be in the middle of a breakup. That hotel made me realize that I had the idea of the marriage but not the intimacy I needed. I wasn't really part of a team. The nostalgia leaves you yearning for more. The idea of a person wraps you up and sometimes you have to unwrap, look inside, and see there's nothing there but your own efforts that fell short. And that's the undeniable truth about being on the road—no matter where you go, there you are.

# DID DREW BARRYMORE TRY TO STEAL MY BOYFRIEND?

Before my ex-husband Matt and I were married, he was my boy-friend and we had just had a baby. The baby was three months old and we were having our first night out at a party. We went big. It was a Halloween party at Drew Barrymore's house. She was a friend of a friend. My costume was "Like a Virgin" Madonna from the eighties. Matt was wearing a onesie-style snowsuit from the seventies that he had gotten at a thrift store. The snowsuit had a couple of electric graphic stripes at the top; the rest of it was bright white and two sizes too small for him, if you know what I mean. Because of him being tall and handsome, the effect was very male stripper.

Her house was in the same neighborhood as the *Playboy* mansion. I heard that it once was owned by Frank Sinatra. The huge gate to the driveway was where you entered, which was in the back of the house. It was large but cozy and one cohesive vibe as soon as you walked in. There was an underground grotto where you could see into the pool. You could look at people while they swam, and allegedly this was a hiding space for gangsters and booze during Prohibition. The dance floor was on a huge driveway next to the pool, and you could walk into the house and straight to the bar. It was a very magical place to be. We were both in high spirits. The party's theme was Alfred Hitchcock's *The Birds*. There were fake crows everywhere and creepy shadowy tree branch lighting. There were so many people in great-looking costumes, and then there was Drew, right in the middle of the dance floor, throwing her hands in the air, having the time of her life.

I was still emotional from being a new mom. I felt clingy but I tried not to show it. I was determined not to let it spoil my good time. I was ready to let loose and have one and a half drinks, dance for three hours, and go home. My fear was that my man would get wasted and want to stay out late or be sloppy and hungover. I don't know why that really mattered, but I guess at the time it was because I was worried we weren't on the same page and he would leave me to party. I was thinking this on the dance floor right when Drew Barrymore danced up to us to say hi. She was mesmerized by his snowsuit and couldn't take her eyes off of him. "Who is this?"

"I'm Matt." Suddenly, no one else existed except for the two of them. Her eyes all over him. I imagined he was used to people reacting with a pause at his good looks. But, if anyone can have anyone's boyfriend at any time, it would be Drew Barrymore. *I* would be her boyfriend if she asked me to. "Nice to meet you," she said, staring into his eyes. I broke her stare by blurting out, "We have a child together!" It came out in a squeal of desperation, like I was trying to sound funny. Even a night of flirting would be too much for me to handle.

I tried to play it off and act cool for the rest of the night. Luckily, Matt didn't go off with her for a make-out session and he managed to have a good time by eventually jumping into the pool with his snowsuit on. As we drove home, I wondered if he knew how scared I was to lose him. Part of it was wondering if I really had him. I didn't know if our bond was strong enough to weather the storms. I held my breath and hoped for the best.

It seemed most likely that he lightly flirted back and let her objectify him because he didn't know what else to do. It's hard to say if I projected my worries onto the entire situation, which was completely innocent.

Just to be on the safe side, when he was sleeping, I picked up the offending snowsuit and threw it in the trash.

# CREATURE COMFORTS

You may imagine I live in the Hollywood Hills with a view of Sunset Boulevard. Or Beverly Hills, walking distance to Rodeo Drive. Let's get serious. I'm more like one really good block in Silver Lake or East Hollywood. Near the gay hair salon, used-clothing store where you can also buy cocaine, and the music school for kids that Flea started. With dive bars, comedy rooms, art galleries. You'd find me hanging out with my friends who are all comedians, writers, actors, and musicians. My Hollywood crew defined me and gave me a career. Being a part of the scene was integral to my life. This was my purpose and reason for living.

In 2015, we moved to Encino, because that's where you go when you're ready to give up. Like "Valley Girl" by Frank Zappa. Or the movie *Encino Man* with Pauly Shore. I gave up on the idea of living in a hot spot to make the inevitable move to suburbia because I now had a husband and a young child.

To get to Encino you get on a beautiful freeway called the 101 and sit there. Take in the traffic. You may even drive through a wildfire. When you see the peaks and valleys have dissipated into a flatland with a hotbed of strip malls replacing cool clubs and restaurants, you've reached your exit.

I had worked really hard to not be living in the suburbs because I know what that life is about: complacency and comfort. But here I was enjoying the quiet, the park nearby, and all of the comforts of having a CVS and a Starbucks nearby. It's very similar to Trenton, Michigan. My parents grew up in downtown Detroit. They were part of the white flight out of Detroit in the few years after the riots in 1967. They had three small girls and didn't want them to be bussed away from their nearby elementary school to another school farther away, so they moved to the newly built houses in Trenton: an unfinished development where the school and park were within walking distance. They also wanted to be closer to my father's job at the power plant in Trenton. I had a nice childhood but there wasn't any diversity or culture. My most valuable experiences came from living in big cities around people who were different than me.

Now, here I was following in their footsteps, creating a comfortable, safe life for my family.

A couple of days after moving in, one of my neighbors, Carol, a white woman in her mid-seventies, came over to say hello. She and her family were from Norway, which sounds really good on paper. She'll probably be cool. The first sentence was nice.

"This is a family neighborhood."

"Great."

"I'm so happy it was a nice family like you all . . ."

"Thanks . . . ?!" What was she saying?

"I'm so relieved. We moved here in the eighties you know, before the Blacks." Holy shit.

And I just stood there listening to her talk about the Blacks and the Hispanics and I didn't say shit. I couldn't correct her. I just thought, *Please God, let her die soon. Let her die right now. I'll call 911.*

"Then after the Blacks came the Hispanics and now they're everywhere. There's a Black family down there. You can't go one block without walking into something."

"Nice to meet you. I've got to go." I waved to her husband.

These are the type of people that will live to be over a hundred. All that bile coursing through their veins keeps them spry. Why did I feel like an asshole? What could I say that would change her nasty, nasty mouth? Nothing. But I could have said something like "You little racist piece of shit. Don't speak to me or anyone like that." But instead, I did nothing. I let her say those things to me. I smiled and backed up into my house like she was holding me at knife point—and I never talked to her again.

Avoidance is my favorite tactic. I'm not proud of it.

We had been in the neighborhood for a few years when a thirty-five-year-old man approached me as I was getting out of my car. I was holding a bag of groceries and he started talking to me like we were old friends. His energy was warm but he was also needy. He wanted to talk.

"Hey, how are you doing?" he asked me.

"I'm good. How are you?"

"I'm doing better because yeah . . . you know, since the stroke. Yeah. I don't know if you remember, I had a stroke."

"What is your name?"

"Paul."

"Oh yeah, sorry. I'm glad you're doing better."

"I mean, I have to walk with this cane now, but I'm just happy to be alive."

"Oh, I'm sure. Congratulations . . ."

"It's a big adjustment. I've had to really slow down. They didn't know if I would walk again or speak. I'm in a lot of therapy. And there's been good days and bad days."

"Wow. That's really hard. I'm really happy for you. It sounds like you're doing an amazing job."

"I used to see you and your husband and your kid walking your dog from my window. I couldn't even say hi because I didn't want to be around your family when I was using." How noble. "I just loved it so much. It was my favorite feeling. Yeah, the crazy part is that it could have been avoided but maybe not. The stroke was induced by my crystal meth use."

"Mm-hmm." The paper grocery bag is losing form from the frozen pizza melting. I try to hold on to the items while also trying to absorb what he's telling me.

"I loved going out to the clubs."

"Yeah."

"Here's the weird part. When I would do crystal meth, it made me want to dress in women's clothes." He laughed. "I don't do that anymore."

"Really?"

"Yeah, I'm sorry. Am I talking too much?"

"No, that's OK. It sounds like you're really processing everything."

"Yeah, I would wear sparkly dresses and put on high heels and makeup. And I was into guys. Like I would do stuff with guys."

"Oh I see."

"Yeah, I don't have those urges now. And my facial hair came back. I feel recovered."

"OK, talk to you later."

The next time I saw . . . oh gosh I had forgotten his name again. The next time I saw him, he was walking down the sidewalk toward me.

He pointed to his shoulder and said, "This is Charlie. He's my best friend."

A rat was sleeping on his collar. He wanted to know if I wanted to hold Charlie. I didn't want to. He described in great detail the way Charlie walks up the stairs and how he can tell when Charlie has to go to the bathroom and when Charlie would like to sit in the sun and how smart he is. He told me that even his mom loves Charlie. That's when I put it together. Racist Carol was his mom.

The next time I saw him, he told me Charlie had died. He was so sad but Carol took it the hardest. She would not stop crying. I pictured Carol in her adult son's room. Both of them not looking at each other but at Charlie the rat on the floor. Mother is crying, loud and ugly in a way she never did about her son. Yelping for air, hugging herself over the dead rat.

"I'm sorry for your loss," I told him.

"I don't know what I'll do without him. Does that sound weird?"

"No, not at all."

We're all just trying to care about something or someone. I felt bad for him, having to learn how to live without Charlie and without meth.

Paul lost Charlie and I lost my friends and hanging out in dive bars in my liberal artsy neighborhood. But I had my family and a sweet little house in the suburbs and luckily I never saw his racist mother again.

# RIP, MY MEMORY

An ex-boyfriend of mine named Josh would always remind me of the things I didn't remember.

"You forgot my birthday again!"

We had a couple of dinners outdoors during COVID. We reminisced about the eight months we were together, in the summer and fall of 2005. He said, "I was in love with you. I proposed but you probably don't remember."

"There was a large lawn near a hill, and you said, 'I love you.' Was that the time? Did you ask me on that lawn?" I said.

"I don't know if there was a lawn," he admitted.

"See you don't remember stuff too." I was vindicated and continued, "I taught you how to ski! Do you remember that? I taught you 'pizza and french fries' like I had seen the ski instructors do with the kids."

"Of course, I remember. Do you remember taking those pills in Joshua Tree, then when you were sleeping you had spasms and I thought you were dying?" Josh said, self-satisfied.

"I don't remember that." I pouted.

This became a competition of "the person who remembers more cares more," and it looks like he won.

My bad memory has served me well. I forgot my cousins taunted me until one day I was in the shower and it popped into my head. Same with the neighbor boy who tackled me and shoved leaves down my shirt to cop a feel (which wouldn't have been that bad except I was pinned to the ground and couldn't breathe). I forget how depressing my grandmother's apartment was. You're not supposed to keep certain things at the forefront of your memory.

I guess I forgot you proposed and you're right. That's all we both needed to know.

I'll admit, sometimes my loss of memory doesn't serve me. The other day my friend Chelsea and I were working on a podcast. I told her, "I want to do a joke about my dog Emily."

"You have done a joke about her."

"No, I mean a short joke I have in mind, not the whole story of her death, which I've talked about."

"You did that joke."

"Maybe I told you the idea but I haven't performed it as a joke on stage."

"That's what I'm talking about."

"A joke? A fully constructed joke?"

"Yes. More than once."

"How is that possible that I wouldn't remember that?!"

"I don't know!"

"What did I say?"

"You said: 'My dog is dying. She is my golden child. For two reasons. One, she brought so much joy in her short cockapoo life and she was also incontinent.' You said it on stage at that show where they bussed in sixteen-year-olds on a field trip."

"Oh yeah. They just stared at me. I remember that show but I still don't remember the incontinence joke. I remember the staff bringing them little bowls of vanilla ice cream during my set."

Why didn't I remember that? I wanted answers. That is a perfectly good double metaphor, one sweet and one savory. A possible beginning into a larger story that I wanted to tell about my beloved blonde cockapoo who is now in doggie heaven. The fact that a person outside of my body can remember my life better than me is a problem? I tell jokes on stage for a living for people who don't see me as a comedian but as the actress from their favorite drama. That's already an uphill battle. If I'm not remembering perfectly good material, it's a detriment to my livelihood. I don't mean to be dramatic, but I feel like this is a house of cards crashing down on me. I'm in the middle of a car crash. What is wrong with me?

I imagine most people wake up in the morning and think, *What do I have to do today?* And then they quickly remember and execute. My memory takes a little longer to warm up. The first thing I think when I wake up is: *Who am I? Am I still here? Do I exist?* That's where I start from. It's hard when you wake up every day with a debilitating condition. You can't begin to work on having a better memory when you're starting by questioning your own existence.

My personality is that of a goldfish. Is my memory problem a psychological avoidance and denial tactic that started as a coping mechanism for something because I needed to escape into a bye-bye world and not hold on to things? Guys, can you imagine if I had a recovered memory right now as I'm writing this? I think it's a form of self-sabotage. I'm refusing to remember. Yeah, maybe. I'm creating this situation for myself where I'm like the guy that pushes the rock up the hill and then it rolls down and then I do it again.

Is it happening right now? Am I forgetting things at this moment? Can I stop it if I want to? Here's what Google says to do:

1. Include physical activity in your daily routine.
I already know how to bench press ten pounds. I think I'm good.

2. Stay mentally active. Try a mentally stimulating activity like a crossword puzzle.
Crossword puzzles are too stressful. I don't like not knowing all the answers instantly.

3. Take alternate routes while driving.
I have the Waze app and it sucks!

4. Learn to play a musical instrument.
I was fifth chair flute in high school band. I didn't care for the waiting. You have to pay attention and wait for the flute part to come in. Then it stops and you do it again with the next song. Not a fan.

5. Volunteer at a local school or community organization.
That's not going to happen. Volunteering stresses me out. One time I volunteered at this place for developmentally disabled adults. It was in San Francisco and I went to teach them how to do artwork. I was a huge fan of their artwork. I was excited to be around the artists and witness them working. Then one guy kept yelling, "Hi, how are you?"

"I'm fine. How are you?"

"How are you today?"

"Really good, thanks."

"How are you today?"

"Um, good?" This went on for forty-five minutes.

Another lady threw paint at me and I apologized to her. She then made fun of me.

I didn't volunteer more than one day there.

6. Socialize regularly.

Usually drink a lot of coffee then talk to my dog and cat. I'm good.

7. Get organized.

My desk is piles of paper. Scraps with numbers, phrases without a context. Bills mixed in with journal writing. Clues to who I am and what my life is. It's like the movie *Memento*.

8. Sleep well.

Is thirteen hours a day good?

9. Eat a healthy diet.

The other day I ate Cinnamon Toast Crunch out of the box with my hand, in a dark corner, so I think I've got this one covered.

It's so important to maintain a balanced outlook on life. I hope these tips have helped some of you as much as they have me.

# HARRISON FORD

After I got the part of Janet, assistant to Harrison Ford's character in the movie *Firewall*, I went into an office building and Harrison Ford was there. It wasn't the audition. We didn't talk about anything. I just said hi. We stood around and they didn't say it explicitly, but I believe that meeting was to make sure that I didn't freak out when I was around him. Clearly, he's not Meredith Baxter Birney, to me at least. But he is Han Solo. By the time I was in this movie I had acclimated to seeing famous people. My new attitude was to be quiet, responsive, and act like they're just people.

Later, during filming, the assistant director had called in a background actor to add more movement into one shot in an office scene. They decided the background player would be an assistant-type person handing Harrison a piece of paper and then continuing down the hallway. He was even given a line. "Here you go, sir. Hello, Janet." They rehearsed it with Harrison Ford's stand-in, and then when it was time to shoot and the background actor got close and tried to hand him the piece of paper, his hand was shaking. It was shaking so badly that he started to smile and giggle uncontrollably.

"Cut!" And that was the last we saw of that background actor. You only get one chance to not freak out around Harrison Ford.

I loved to be around him. He was funny and gruff but kind of humble. Present but also over it. The first time I saw him on set, he walked on and immediately started talking over the director. He was changing the shot to how he thought it would work better. That's what you do when you're Harrison Ford.

Later, I saw him at craft services. He had his head down and was just making that tough decision between trail mix and corn nuts. Or maybe it was an M&Ms moment. Tough call. You really need to space out the snacking over the twelve hours you'll be on set. Sometimes I snack so much that I can't eat the meal. I tried to not notice him because I imagine his life was people being hyper-focused on him even in small mundane moments where no one should be noticing (exactly what I was doing).

On the day of the snacks I sat next to Mr. Ford on a cement bench outside, and I believe we had a very brief conversation about God. I'd like to believe that he adopted a Buddhist type of belief system, you know, like wise people do. I remember being able to sit close to him and talk about something deep and eternal, but totally normal, for maybe three minutes.

I had never been on a mega action movie set like that, and I couldn't believe how long it took to light. Even indoors in a completely contained situation, it took hours and hours to do one tiny scene. I had one line and it took all of my energy just to not pass out from boredom. Hours would pass and then I'd have to get back into the scene where I needed to smile while standing on that mark, say the one thing and then turn my head and sit down. It was so numbing to have to go back and make that line seem natural after we had been working on this one part of one scene for what seemed like years. If I had an actual scene with more words, it was almost easier to get going. You get past the amount of time that you waited and then you're in the scene and you can have fun once you're in the scene. But when you have to wait and wait and wait, then, "You're on!," it's hard. You can't ramp into it. You just have to be on all at once and then nothing, nothing, nothing, nothing, nothing for so long. So it became an exercise in how to do that.

On the other hand, I was also lucky enough to have quite a few scenes with Harrison Ford, who played a banker forced by criminals to use his inside access to steal money. When he tries to get out of it, he ends up more deeply under the control of the criminals and then they move into his house and hold his wife and kids hostage. The bad guys assume his identity to make it look to others like he is stealing money. So, no one trusts him and everyone thinks he's a criminal and losing his mind. His character turns to his assistant at the bank, Janet. That's me. Janet is the only one who can potentially still help him.

He shows up at my funky downtown apartment, which in real life was a sketchy place. It was a rent-by-the-hour hotel in downtown Vancouver! OK, it was actually an extended-stay hotel for transients. There were needles, alcohol, and prostitutes there, but production dressed it up to look cute! They painted the dreary apartment a fun color, and you know Janet put a colorful scarf over a lamp because she was a poor single woman trying to rise above the patriarchy.

My hair was styled in braids. Braids are not a good hairstyle for me. The hair department was really working overtime trying to win that Oscar. If you go back and watch the movie, each hairstyle of mine was worse than the next. Weird teasing, mysterious parts, and colorful streaks that show up out of nowhere. Again, to show what a charming personality poor Janet has. The braids were the best hairstyle and they were bad.

Anyway, now he's at my door, this big strong man trying to save his family—so intense, it's some real Indiana Jones shit! Yes! I scream (as Janet) because the last time I saw him, he was unhinged and fired me. Remember the plot of the movie, guys. I open the door. I see it's him. I scream. He bangs on the door again. He pushes the door open and covers my mouth so that I don't scream. His character is frantic. He grabs me on the shoulders and pushes me on the couch. If you ask me it was a pretty hard push. He said something to the director which, in my opinion, acknowledged that he manhandled me. He was like, "Oh, we should get her a massage."

It was exhilarating to be pushed around by Harrison Ford. Doesn't make it right. But you know, I kind of loved it. I remember thinking, *Holy shit. How is this happening?*

Then there was another part that I remember. We are in the car together. He is driving. As soon as the camera can't see him, he stops the car. The action isn't over. The car still needs to drive a hundred feet or so, but Harrison Ford is done being in the scene. He gets out of the car and *he takes me with him!* The crew knows that it's time for the stand-in to do the rest of the drive. Never in my career have I not been a "team player" and done the long shot, the insert of my hand. The deep background where you may see my shoulder, the back of my head. Getting to exit that car as soon as we were out of focus was some big movie star shit. It was heaven. I just giggled my way through that shit. I felt like a million bucks and like Harrison Ford's buddy.

In our final car scene together, Harrison Ford's character has just remembered his dog has a tracking chip, so he logs into the dog-tracking website and we use it to follow his family. We were filming in a place called Kamloops, British Columbia. We all drove through this beautiful, mountainous, lush area to get to the shooting location. I remember being there with the crew waiting on Harrison. He was late.

We started filming and I was driving the car because it was my character's car. I was in this car in close proximity to him and we have a walkie-talkie to the rest of the world outside the car. We were driving down this windy road that would lead us to the dog. When we got to the starting place of the action at the top of the hill, we could see the dog down the road, accompanied by his dog handler.

From what I can remember, the conversation went something like this:

"Jesus Christ! Not her," he said. I burst out laughing.

"You don't like the handler."

"Ugh, I just don't want her to talk to me. It's a dog. I know how to pick up a dog!"

"Maybe she has a special way . . ."

"Fuck her . . ." He may have said this.

I laughed. I believed he was being extra faux-angry to make me laugh, but I really didn't know. He was being funny. If he hated the dog handler, I hated her too. Harrison Ford shit-talking the dog handler is a career highlight for me. I always told myself to have reverence for people who had a certain specialty. Let them do their thing and say their rules. It's up to me to bite my tongue and get through it.

"What does she need to tell me about picking up a dog?!" Great point. I did not know the answer.

After this scene, we were to have a few days off.

It was a Friday morning and he said to me, "Are you going home this weekend?"

I laughed. "Yeah . . . no, I'm not."

"Do you want a ride back to LA?"

"Yes?" I wasn't sure what he meant but I said yes.

"We'll leave on Friday morning. I'll send a car for you." It was then I realized he meant I could ride back on his plane with him. Now I was nervous. What if he was piloting? What if he wasn't and I had to make one-on-one conversation outside of the set? Being on a private plane with Harrison Ford is not an everyday moment, but there was no one to ask. I suddenly thought I needed an outfit and a bag, so I went to the mall and bought a really stylish, expensive carry-on bag and a blouse. I wanted to look like I belonged on a private jet.

I ultimately realized that he was simply extending the ride, which is beyond amazing.

I remember having to stop for customs but when you're on Harrison Ford's plane, you make an extra stop and then the customs officers come to you.

Two customs officers in their early twenties were giggling and apologizing and walked onto the plane and said, "Um, can we see your passports?" And then they left and we took off again.

When I got back to LA, there was a car waiting for me. I couldn't freak out and say, "This is the most amazing experience of my life!" I just acted like it was normal and I said, "Thank you! Have a great weekend"

"You too." No big deal.

After the movie came out, I even had the pleasure of having an award presented to me by Harrison Ford. I can't remember what the award is. That's just how I roll. It was some newcomer breakout thing from a magazine, and they actually got Harrison to present it to me!

I remember being at the party after the screening of *Firewall*. There was a lot of congratulating about what a fantastic job we all did. It was wrong—the movie wasn't good. It was confusing and built suspense at the wrong times. The pace was off and the story seemed to be missing parts. There were too many cooks in the kitchen trying to do too many things.

I realized that someone needed to tell Harrison Ford. He's surrounded by yes men. I was his buddy and it was my moral obligation to let him know. I waited for the right moment and then I whispered in his ear, "This is not a good movie." This was not a good choice in my life. I'm not proud of doing this. I regret doing this, but I guess at the very least I can admit it here.

He stared at me not knowing what to say. I drifted off into the party and never flew on his private plane again.

# AN ACTING LESSON FROM KIEFER

There was a hierarchy on *24*. I had my place. I wanted to do well and not get in the way (my mantra for life). I tried to be present but steer clear of direct, prolonged contact. That in itself could be a certain kind of friendship. My perception is that Kiefer appreciated me as I was—I was there to do my job and not be up in his grill.

There were times during a scene where there was a genuine exchange of energy, a communication that was listening and reacting. This is called acting. There were a few moments in scenes with him that are some of my best life memories.

In one particular episode, I was called to act in a scene with a blank screen. I had already done a bit of this, having been hired to play a computer genius. I was comfortable using my computer as a prop while talking to other characters. This time it was different because the scene was longer and it involved feelings. When the director said, "Action," I was going to need to instantly be very upset, and I was scared I didn't know how to do it. The scene called for me to be watching my friend who was miles away being attacked, via a security camera.

It was a scene where I was watching footage of a friend trying to ride away from terrorists on his bike. He gets pulled off his bike and beaten.

On the day we were to shoot the scene, there were two large cameras fixed on me ready to go. There was a quick rehearsal for lighting and composition. (There wasn't any dialogue to rehearse!) When I walked away, they began to light the set. I started to panic. I wasn't able to get emotional at all during rehearsal, and rehearsal was about ten seconds, just long enough for them to check the camera position. I had about fifteen minutes to figure out how to instantly become emotional in response to something specific but invisible. The more I worried, the less "in the zone" I was. I didn't know how to get in my body and find my emotions.

I saw Kiefer in the hair and makeup trailer getting ready for the next scene. Normally I was too intimidated to talk to him, but I was in a real pickle and needed help. I didn't want to take up his time or insult him but also didn't want to do a bad job in the scene. So, I took a chance and said, "I'm about to do the scene where I'm watching Andrew get pulled to the ground and beaten; I don't know how to do it."

"What do you mean?" he said.

"The screen is blank, what am I supposed to do?"

"It's a series of reactions..."

"Yes."

He took a look at my face as I started to crumble in fear.

"To no one and nothing." I was being petulant because I didn't know any other way to express myself.

"Yeah, those are tricky. I can help you," he said.

"Really, are you sure?" I was being midwestern over-apologetic and acting as if I didn't want to put him out. He gave me a look that said, "Of course." He followed me to set and when it was time to shoot, he stood off to the side and read the stage directions that explained what was happening. He then started improvising what I was seeing, so I could react to it. "He fell off his bike. They're on him now. They hit him. He's on the ground covering his head. It's not clear how badly he's been hurt." Simple but extremely helpful.

I was very fortunate to once again be able to learn on the job. It was probably nothing to him, but it has stayed with me all these years.

# HOW TO MAINTAIN YOUR DIGNITY

Today, my lunch is out of the vending machine. I chose two bags of Snyder's Pretzel Pieces and two packages of Little Debbie Peanut Butter Bars. I'm in Butte, Montana.

The café that I walk to for my big breakfast that gets me through the day is closed. Everything is closed. It's two degrees outside. The fake-nice production assistants usually rattle the cages (our rooms where we're quarantined) by leaving food outside the door at three thirty P.M. and nine thirty P.M. Production is on nights; so far, the movie has been only night shoots. I haven't been on set yet, so I'm still on a regular person's daily feeding schedule. But the night shoots mean breakfast is at three thirty P.M. It's Eggos and sausage crumpled up in a small Styrofoam to-go container, with maple-flavored corn syrup on the side. I asked the delicate little bird where I could get a bottle of water and a coffee. She said she would bring me some and then two hours later she said, "I don't have it."

"I guess I will be walking in two-degree weather, point eight miles down the freeway to the only café I can see that is open."

"But it's two degrees out," the little bird said, dropping the nice facade.

"I know but I don't know what else to do. I can drink tap water but I really would also like a tea or a coffee. I can do it. It's just double the distance I went yesterday in the same weather. I need to be careful because there's a layer of ice under the snow and it's next to the freeway. But by the time I get there, does the experience of having a tea get canceled out by the thirty-minute walk in ice and wind? Food and water are such First World problems, right?" She had a horrified look on her face, not sure if I was serious or not. I was not sure either.

"You can borrow my hat and my gloves. Just give them back at some point." She laughed uncomfortably and handed me her dingy pink fuzzy set. This was a new low for me, borrowing the hat and gloves of a hard-working production assistant on a low-budget movie. It made her feel better to offer me her stuff because she didn't have any access to coffee, and this was a way she could help. I smiled wanly and took her hat and gloves as I considered taking the walk. Eventually, I would get a hold of the producers and one of them would bring me coffee in his personal cup that he made in his room, with the French press he brought. Now I know to add "access to coffee" in my contracts.

I could hear voices through the walls of the hotel. All the people I didn't know who were working on this movie. Gossiping, scampering around. They came alive around six P.M. I learned the director likes nights because it "feels different." She's filming all the scenes at night, even scenes that are indoors and would be so easy to shoot during the day. This is an odd sadomasochistic choice. She was twenty-three years old, making an artistic feature about violence, sex, and gender roles. I was now subject to her whims, to her creative process. It was upon learning this that I began to question my choice to say yes to this film.

When I made the decision to come here, I wasn't a victim. I was large and in charge, an artist who had some free time and was looking for a change of pace. But now, it seemed my fresh attitude was about to get its comeuppance. I sat in my hotel room alone, no contact with the outside world. The overheard voices in the walls of the other crew members would keep me company when I could no longer scroll Twitter.

This is an independent low-budget movie. The character is a butch lesbian. Fun! One scene. Easy peasy. The fantasy is that the scene I play in will be so layered and nuanced, they will say, "We have to give her the Oscar for best seven lines in an obscure queer-centric film!" I will bring depth and emotion and understanding to this character relating to this other character. I mean, no one will see this movie, it might never come out, and chances are I won't actually even see the final product. But, hey, that's the life of an artist! There is an adventure ahead to meet people and see how they work, and it didn't hurt when my agent said, "It's a straight offer!" which means I didn't have to audition, which is the best.

Plus, Demi Moore is doing it. You heard me right. Drop everything. This is the type of name recognition that makes business-people believe, "This is a good project. This could get made. People might actually watch it." Demi can make it happen.

When I saw my travel itinerary, I noticed it was on Frontier Airlines. My gut said, *This can't be good.* Then I wondered, *Is this a real airline?* The message was: This is what we can afford. I laughed to myself, *I guess I'll be flying Frontier for the first time in my life because I am nothing if not a team player.*

On the way to the airport I got a burst of hopeful, excited energy, like, *Hey, anything is possible, the road is open.* At the airport, I started to get nervous. There were more people than I thought there would be considering the pandemic, and I hadn't been on an airplane since the COVID-19 outbreak. What if the militia took over the airport and I got stranded? My nerves were worked up so I drank a beer. I sat on the floor next to an outlet with my mask and clear plastic face shield as far away from people as possible. Nearby was a MAGA couple also sitting on the floor next to an outlet. The woman had frizzy hair and her vibe was "I'm on pills." The man was loud (shocking) and he was explaining to her how the world works; he was really throwing his dick around about counting votes and socialism. Ten minutes until boarding turned into twenty minutes going on an hour and they weren't telling us why the flight was delayed.

People lined up in a close group to get their questions resolved. I didn't want to stand in line because of COVID. After an hour, I stood in line. No one was giving us any information. Suddenly three hours after the original boarding time, we were told the plane was ready to take off. So I made it to Denver but of course missed my connection to my destination: Butte, Montana.

I called Frontier Airlines and the lady kept asking me why I missed my connecting flight and I kept telling her Frontier had missed my departing flight. "I need a new connecting flight, what can't you understand?"

I hung up with her because I made it to the front of the line and I could talk to the Frontier employee in front of me. They told me that they wouldn't book my connecting flight.

"Our next flight to Butte is two weeks from now."

"No, I'm trying to make the connection, which I missed because the flight was late. Can you help me?"

"Yes, in two weeks."

"What do you mean? I'm trying to make my connection today. The one that I booked."

"Oh, I can only book you on a Frontier flight. We can't book other airlines. I can give you a refund."

"A refund? So, if you guys cancel the flight, I'm just supposed to stay here in Denver for two weeks until the next Frontier flight?! I don't understand."

"What can't you understand?"

"You just made me miss my connection."

"Your refund will arrive in eight to ten days."

"Oh, OK . . . so where would you recommend I book another flight?"

"United."

"Do you know where that is?" She directed me and in the meantime production booked me on a United flight. I needed to go out to baggage claim to get my bag and go back through security. Production sent me the ticket confirmation but my phone was dead. I was also thirsty and hungry and had to go to the bathroom. I was sweating from running back and forth, and my shield was fogging up so I couldn't wear my glasses. After I got my bag I figured the best use of time was to get through United security, look up the flight on the screen, guess which one it was, find the gate, and then charge my phone to see if I was correct. I was able to charge my phone in the gate long enough to pull up my ticket confirmation and make it on the plane. The way things were going, I was worried there might be a problem with my ride. So I texted my driver before the plane took off. His name was Mark.

"My flight is about to leave and my phone will die soon so hopefully I will be able to find you. I am wearing a houndstooth blazer [by J.Crew] and white tennis shoes, and am carrying a hard case lavender roller bag and am wearing a mask and face shield. My name is Mary Lynn. I hope this is the right number."

He said, "On my way to pick you up right now, I got this am reliable will take good care of you and make sure you arrive to Butte safely cannot leave the vehicle unattended however so you will have to manage outside to curb on your own, okay?" This is my kind of run-on sentence. I don't know how to curb on my own but thank you, Mark, for being my beacon of hope. I followed up with "Sure, what kind of car do you have?"

"White Chrysler Pacifica Minivan." It's called communication and we were doing it. Mark met me at the airport wearing pleated jeans with a large belt buckle and a flat top. Within four minutes of meeting Mark, he told me that he was a former navy seal, so he doesn't take crap from people. He said that's why the movie production gave him the job of being the person to enforce mask wearing. He was demoted when he was too strict about enforcing the mask-wearing policy to one of the actors.

"This guy was so dramatic and didn't want to ruin his makeup with the mask. So I told him, 'Well, you're going to ruin it by crying.' That's when they fired me. And you know, these actor guys are so whiny, they're so dramatic, you know who are actually the strongest ones on set? The women! Can you believe it?!"

"Yes Mark, I can."

"All the guys on this set are such babies. That's where the bad behavior is coming from."

"Mark, they should have put you in charge of everything."

"Well, I'm better off being a driver, but then they tried to not pay me what they told me they would pay me!"

"Really?"

"Yeah, they said I'd be making 150 bucks per day as a driver, I said OK and then they come back and say I'm not going to get paid that. You can't do that!"

"That's fucked up, Mark. You're worth at least 150 per day." Then he asked me if it was OK if he stopped for a coffee at McDonald's. I figured I could eat McDonald's, which was better than no food.

"Coffee? How long is the ride?"

"An hour and a half." This trip kept giving and giving.

We drove through at McDonald's and they didn't have any coffee. There was a grocery store across the street that was still open. It was just before ten P.M. We went in and had a very similar trajectory. Somehow I spoke with him like we were a couple.

"Mark, there's Starbucks cold brew in that case if you want it, I don't think I'll get coffee." Next thing you knew he was next to me at the fruit shelves saying, "Oh, healthy! Maybe *I'll* get fruit." We also looked at a humongous selection of kombucha together.

"You like kombucha, Mark?!"

"Yeah, maybe I'll get this."

When we were back in the car, he offered me some tangerines and then we drove for a while in silence. Finally he said, "I'm not afraid of dying. I kind of want to, you know. Just to see what's on the other side." He had a smile on his face while looking straight ahead with his hands at ten and two.

"Mark, don't say that!"

"It's a good thing to say. I am in touch with my own mortality."
Suddenly I was attracted to Mark. This was such a thoughtful statement. His Costco plaid was looking Gucci.

"I guess you're right, that's assuming that you will have your
same consciousness after you die." I wanted to show Mark that I
could hang with this convo.

"A good friend of mine who is a musician says when he dies,
he wants to go to a jazz bar, a midtown jazz bar like where John
Coltrane would be, and stay there." Now he was back into a macho
zone. I was still very into the conversation, his lilting tone, and
responsible nature.

"What happens if you're tired of being in the bar and you want
to go home?" He didn't have an answer and was still very excited
about the places he'd go.

"Imagine smoking a cigar with Ernest Hemingway."

"Eh. . ." I shrugged. "Not my type."

"Anyway, that's the kind of stuff you think about when you live
in Montana. Lotta space out here. Wide-open space to think . . ." I
didn't come up with where I would want to hang out after death,
but the conversation made me feel like I was at home right where
I was. For a few moments, on the dark road to Butte, I felt safe
and satisfied.

I checked into my hotel just before midnight and went right to
sleep. Two hours later, I got a call waking me up saying production
was shutting down because someone got COVID. The assistant
director told me not to worry because we would resume shooting
on Monday. It was Thursday and I was scheduled to fly back on Sun-
day. You see what happened there? She glossed right over the part
where I wouldn't be flying home and I'd be staying to work. She
said they were hoping this individual's test was a "false positive." I

wasn't even sure if that was a thing. I did a lot of "huh?" and "OK" and then spent the next two hours wondering, *What have I done? I don't want to have COVID alone in this hotel room. I don't want to die in Montana. I don't want to say goodbye to my son over FaceTime.*

The COVID Compliance Lady came up the next day to give me a test. She watched me spit into a tube. She said she got to watch Demi Moore spit into a tube too. Neat! She then went on to tell me she respects me and she doesn't respect the producers. She wasn't sure if they were handling this correctly and that their priority was to get the movie made. I appreciated her candor but wasn't sure how worried I should be. All producers pretend to care about you while really you're a prop and they just want to get their movie made. That's pretty normal—maybe she just hadn't been around a lot of producers.

I took a walk around Butte, posting on Instagram. My old friend Fred Armisen texted to say he was enjoying my posts of all the old buildings in Butte. I told him it was a really neat place but I was alone walking on an isolated street when I found out the election results. I texted him: "Now, I am alone in a hotel room in Butte, watching people celebrate on the streets. I'm questioning my life choices. I don't know why I said yes to this movie."

"I am alone in a hotel room in Vancouver. You're like me, you choose art first. I would have done the same thing."

I looked at my welcome email from the producers. "Hello, from your producers! We're so glad you made it here despite the nightmare travel day you had (ugh!) and now this COVID hiccup! What a perfect storm. We'd love to say hi at a safe distance lol and send you a bottle of wine or two. Best, Larry, Makeila and Kev." I'm not sure if COVID is the type of "hiccup" that a bottle of wine can smooth over . . .

The next couple of days, I walked around Butte, scrolling Twitter endlessly and treating myself to egg, bacon, hash browns, and toast breakfasts. On the second morning, I was having the same thing I had the first morning, two eggs, while watching the election count on my laptop, when the lady at the café said, "Can I just say I think that what you do is so inspiring. You're making a movie here?"

"Yeah, I was supposed to be here for a couple of days. One scene, in and out but you know, now there's a COVID scare and a snowstorm. So I'm here in my tennis shoes!"

"You don't have boots?"

"No, I'm from California."

"You didn't pack boots?"

"I was supposed to be back home already. In and out. And it pays scale."

"What's scale?"

"Very little."

When I woke up the next morning, the temperature had dropped twenty degrees. I put on all of the clothes I packed and walked to the café. It was closed. I kept walking, looking for a store to get water but the only one I found was a liquor store. I saw a sign in white and red that said "Food Store." When I went in, there were mostly empty shelves, with some Pringles and Cheetos on one side and on the other there were animals being skinned and sliced. Also, lots of strapping young men in blood-spattered white aprons with big knives.

Then production got pushed again. I decided I needed to get out of there. I texted Fred, "I'm bailing!" We got into a conversation and once I started texting him all the things that happened, I couldn't stop.

"The fourth dinner was nachos made with ground beef and Velveeta, served in Styrofoam!"

"I have to go to the lobby to open a Google Doc!"

"The hotel is haunted!"

"There was hair in the shower. Was it the ghosts'?"

"The producers emailed me: 'Sorry about the COVID hiccup.' "

With three pushes and now being told I'd work tomorrow night, I couldn't take it anymore. I emailed the producers and let them know that I had to go. I wrote, "This situation isn't working for me. I will need to take the scheduled flight back to LA tomorrow. Can you please call my agent and manager to discuss?" Ten minutes later, one of the producers, Ted, called.

"Hey, wanted to let you know that we are definitely on track now. And the good news is your call time will be earlier. Around two P.M.! Isn't that great, and to give you a lay of the land, Demi's scene will be up first—she is on board with all of the changes—and the sound guy who was infected with COVID has been ejected from the set. So we have replaced the sound engineer but there was another person in the sound department who had a personal tragedy, his brother-in-law committed suicide." I surprised myself by not playing into what he was trying to do.

I interrupted him and said, "I get it, Ted, it's hard. It's been really hard on everyone and there are things that happened that have to be dealt with and I am a team player but this was too much for me. Being here was not good for me personally, financially, and it isn't good for my health either, so can you please call my agent to discuss this further."

I told my agent my plan. She was worried. She said, "Are you sure? I don't want you to ruin any relationships."

"What relationship do I have? The one where they pay the bare minimum so I can sit and starve in a hotel room while my only information is what I can hear from production assistants through the walls? Because that's what our relationship is now, so there's nothing to ruin!"

"I guess I can tell them you're worried about COVID . . ."

"That's one worry, but that's not really the point. Did you hear the stuff I just said about the way I'm being treated?"

"Everyone is in the same boat."

"I'm not everyone. I'm in this boat and I don't want to be." Independent moviemaking is not glamorous. This was a bad choice for me. I told my agent if they paid me for another week, I would stay and do the scene.

They agreed. I regretted my decision. Even one more week of pay didn't make it worth my time. What's a little money twice? Still not enough money. They honored my request after trying to ignore me and make assumptions. Now I had to do it and they were forced to treat me with some decency not because they wanted to but because I made them. I also made my agent represent me properly. Once I spoke my truth, I believed it.

We shot the next night in an abandoned building in downtown Butte. The basement was set-dressed as a movie theater. My costume was a men's suit, tie, and shoes from the fifties. Once I met some other people on the crew, I got confirmation that everyone was having the same shitty experience with the lack of communication from the producers. Word on the street was that even Demi was dropped in a hotel room without any welcome or any tips on where to go to get the necessities. This made me feel better in some ways, and I was happy to be around all the creative people who love doing what they do.

In the middle of the night on set, one of the producers, wearing a couture large white puffy winter coat and AirPods, crossed into my path and offered me tea.

"I'm good." I smiled.

"You sure, can I get you some tea?"

I looked two feet to my left, at an electric tea kettle, cups, and tea that had been put out. "I'm good."

We shot the scene and twelve hours later I was on a Delta flight (because I demanded not to fly Frontier) on my way back to LA. When my flight touched down, I received a reply from Fred regarding all the details to which he said, "Well, I didn't know all of that was happening. And Frontier Airlines?! I would have left the first day."

# SECOND CHANCES

After my husband and I divorced in 2020 and my dog had died, my twelve-year-old son picked out our new dog from the Rockin' Rescue website. I wasn't ready for a dog. I was still grieving the loss of my cockapoo, Emily. "That's your dog, Mom," he said.

I said, "No, I'm not ready."

"That's your dog, Mom."

"Really? Why?" I wasn't even sure if I could get on board with their cutesy website: "Help a dog find their furr-ever home."

"It just is," he said. It was the cutest golden retriever mix, sitting straight up with a big smile on his face. I would learn that he was also part crazy. We found out that Leo had knocked over a small child and the family who had adopted him gave him back. My son's joke is that he killed a toddler. Three weeks, two walks, and one home visit later we had that dog. The first day, he attached to me right away. He was large and on the bed on his back looking for belly rubs. Then he would sneeze everywhere. Turns out sneezing is his love language.

Those first few days he wasn't sure what to do with his body in the space. He was very nervous. He chewed through bones, toys, blankets, pillows, and cardboard. I stayed in the bedroom with him. I brought an "animal expert" to meet him so I could address the chewing and anxiety. He growled at her. It was me, him, and all his hair up in the bedroom. Then there was our cat, who was outside the bedroom door. The real boss of the house. After a few days, they were allowed to view each other through a screen that I put up in the bedroom door. The cat methodically licked the screen to get his scent on it. It was his way of dominating the house. It was a sight to behold. I respect his game. After five days of slowly letting the cat and dog meet each other, they were best friends.

Leo doesn't like it when people hug. If someone comes over and I hug them hello, he will bark aggressively. The sounds of nail clippers, scissors, and laughter drive him crazy. He doesn't like when I do jumping jacks or run in place. One time my friend was helping me decorate and when she moved a plant he lunged at her. He does not like change or excitement or mystery sounds. He is stubborn. If he doesn't want to do something, he will plant himself down with all of his might and it is impossible to move him.

I needed to find a new groomer because he wouldn't let mine cut his hindquarters or his nails. I saw this mobile grooming truck and thought I'd give it a try. When the guy arrived, he had a hat, apron, gloves, and a mask. Leo did not want to go near him at all. This guy, Asan, told me he was spiritually connected and had a deep understanding of animals. He recommended I give Leo CBD pills and then said he would come back another time and he was sure he could get Leo on the truck to groom.

A week later, I was walking Leo through some grass on the shoulder of the road near my house when I saw a book on the ground. Someone had dropped the Quran. I was startled. Ancient holy scriptures on the ground! I couldn't leave it, so I picked up the wet holy book and took it home. When I got back from the walk, I left the wet book, my shoes, and the leash on the porch to dry out and walked inside to find a towel to dry my dog's paws and forgot about the book.

A few more days passed and Asan came back to groom Leo. Asan promised that he really understood dogs, and this time he knew Leo would be more comfortable with him. When Leo caught sight of Asan he planted himself and growled, baring his teeth. Somehow, Asan continued to explain to me dog behavior and how all dogs love him.

We ended up near the porch where Asan noticed the book on the ground. He stopped talking and slowly looked down. He leaned toward the book and said, "Do you mind?"

"No, not at all. It's a Quran. I found it on the ground."

He stared at the book in disbelief. Again he said, a little more sternly this time, "Do you mind? This is a holy book. It is a great offense to me that it is on the ground. Can you pick it up, please?"

I instantly found myself trying to smooth things over, "Oh, sure yeah. OK. Let me go ahead and put that in the house." I wanted to say: "I picked it up off the *ground*, asshole!" He needed to talk to the guy who dropped it in the first place! Asan said he was willing to come again to try to groom Leo.

"No, thanks. I think we should call this off."

"If you get the CBD oil and give it to your dog, like I mentioned before I think this will be a lot easier. Trust me, I know when dogs are stressed—"

"That's great but I just don't think this is working. Thank you for trying." Asan took the rejected Quran and left, taking with him an idea that I was out to blaspheme his religion and his God. It was probably better this way.

# MY FAVORITE LAVANDERÍA

The house in Encino was the last place we lived together as a family. It had a small yard with a pool and a barbecue grill that my husband bought. I bought and paid for the house, he got the grill. It was near the park. This is where we were creating the story of our family. It became the place I would come home to after being on the road doing stand-up for the weekend and my husband would be staring at the TV. When I asked how his weekend was, "nothing" had happened and his manner and tone let me know I was bothering him by asking. A couple of years after we got divorced, he told me that he never liked to have other people in his space.

In that house, our sex life dwindled. In that house, he had an office where he would spend hours learning how to buy crypto currency. He had to get some really fat cable for the internet. Extreme Wi-Fi! The office had a huge desk that he needed, a foot massager, and a two-thousand-dollar recliner from the "Relax the Back" store. There was always some ailment that he would try to fix, always something that wasn't right and that kept him from me. He seemed to be imprisoned in his own mind and I thought I could unlock the cell. This was foolish on my part. He let me know that he was overwhelmed. He didn't really have much time to connect because he was busy trying to get ahead in his business. I would ask if he wanted to have breakfast or take our kid to school together on mornings that allowed for that. He didn't have the time.

I tried to not take it personally that he didn't want to be around me. I knew he loved me. I loved him the best I could. We had lived in the house five years, since 2015. Our son was eleven and after the divorce, I was going to keep the house because I loved it. When COVID took over our lives, I had to cancel my next few months of personal appearances and come to terms with the fact that I was always waiting to share bills with Matt. My life had become more modest, but I was still always waiting for the next big job to make it through the next month. It was time to give up the dream and downsize again. My real estate agent told me that in order to sell my house, I'd need to move out so he could fix it up to sell. So, I took my son and the dog and cat and moved into an overpriced Cozy (Cockroach Infested) Cottage Airbnb that has no laundry amenities. The goal was to afford the ability to create a little cocoon for myself where I could keep my son in a good school, work on my art, and still remain in the city that I love.

My son didn't like the Airbnb. The rooms were funky. The walls and floors were uneven, the furniture was mismatched, and, of course, the cockroaches. It was small and dusty and the box air conditioning went out. The landlord came over to ask if I rinsed out the filter. I said yes but she did it again anyway and then declared it fixed. There's one bedroom, which is fine. They allow a dog and a cat and it's two miles from the old house and Dad's condo. It's exactly what I need during this transition.

"I want to sleep at Dad's," my son said. *What do you mean you don't want to stay here? My whole reason for being is you.* I don't say that. I just say, "OK." The one night I did convince him to stay, I gave him the bedroom and stayed in the living room drinking wine and watching *Peaky Blinders*. I slept on the couch. Every twenty minutes when one arm would fall asleep, I would roll to my other side like a pork chop cooking all night long. After that night he never stayed again. I don't even think he saw a cockroach that night, so I'm not sure what the problem was. I didn't like not being home base. I wanted to have the family house while Dad was in his bachelor condo. Now the condo was the home base while I stayed in the cockroach cottage.

The Airbnb didn't have a washing machine. At first, I would drive to my house, which was getting ready to go on the market, and do my laundry there. But that option didn't last long. I was in the way of the handymen and the house stager, which is probably for the best because I would cry every other time I entered the house, telling myself each time that the crying was me saying a final goodbye to the house and that time of my life but then crying again on my next visit. Also my dog, who loves walks and car rides, would refuse to come into the house. He knew something was up.

My ex-husband has a washer and dryer that I half pay for. Why don't I just do my laundry there, you ask? I tried. We got into a fight that was completely started, middled, and ended by me after drinking one rum and ginger ale. I was trying to get into party mode. We had agreed to watch a movie while I did my laundry. We were watching *Terminator 2* and at a certain point my son said, "What world are the robots from?" and wondered if they had already been mentioned in the movie. "I think it's another model and that—" He wasn't interested in my answer. He interrupted me to say, "Dad, what world are the robots from?"

"What?" His dad was in the kitchen and wasn't even paying attention, but he would rather get his opinion than mine. I gave my son a dirty look. He knew it was over. But I was just getting started. When I opened my mouth, the train was already way off the tracks. "I'm not going to be shooed away like a fly. Why am I even here if no one wants to be around me?!" It was an overreaction to a moment that had already passed, but once I got going I couldn't stop. "I won't be treated like this. Like I don't matter and my thoughts are worthless. I'm the one who keeps this whole family together so don't treat me like that! I'm going to go."

"Don't go, Mom." I got up in a huff and checked my laundry and my clothes weren't even halfway through the wash cycle. I started to yank them out but they were too wet, so I began putting them back in.

"My clothes aren't done, so I guess I'm staying!"

My ex-husband was ignoring the situation and waiting for it to go away, as per usual, while my son got angry. He went to his room and slammed the door. I followed him, opening his door yelling, "You don't get to be mad at me for getting mad at you! I'm the one who is being treated like crap! Now, let's watch the rest of the movie!" We never finished watching that movie. I left and my ex-husband put my laundry in the dryer and I picked it up later.

I had to go to a laundromat. No big deal. Actually, I really enjoy the experience of being at a laundromat when I am on location working. You have none of the responsibilities of being at home and when you're a smaller character, you have less to do and lots of days off. While working in Atlanta I went to this laundromat that has bright orange walls and Salvador Dalí posters on the wall. I love that place. I would hang out there even if I had no laundry.

There's a laundromat 0.3 miles away from the Airbnb. I'll pretend I'm on location. It will be fun. I gave myself enough time to start a load before I went to pick up my son for the day. The machine wouldn't start. You gotta be freaking kidding me. I do the whole setup again with a second machine. That doesn't work either! So I really concentrate, really focus on the buttons to make sure I'm doing every step. Third one same thing. I'm starting to get a little panicky and feel my throat tightening up. I ran out of there.

A few days later after I had recovered, I found another laundromat. The machines worked! I started the machines and made my way across the street. There was a bakery. "Oh, is that a pupusa?" I asked. No one answered. I could feel the surge of hungry workers pushing me forward. Operation breakfast was running like clockwork. "Buenos días" this and "Gracias" that. People talking in some kind of code. I couldn't crack it. The cashiers seemed to know everyone's order. I didn't have the time to smell or do a taste test. And my eyeballs couldn't quickly discern what was what. Before I knew it, the line had spit me out the door with just a coffee.

On the positive side, as I walked back to the *lavandería* I got catcalled by the drunk guys outside. I've still got it. I walked past them twice so they could take a look at the flip side. Get a good look at it! They also allowed dogs at the laundromat, so I was able to bring my dog, Leo, with me. Having my dog made an older gentleman think that was an invitation to talk. "Beautiful dog," he said.

"Thank you."

"What's his name?"

"Leo."

"Like the lion."

I fake laughed. "Yep."

"I wrote a screenplay about a dog. They made it into a movie!"

"Oh really?" Here we go . . .

"It was about a dog named Vince who dreams he was a human and then he sets out to find out if it's true in his waking life. People loved it. It was actually pretty funny too. But I didn't get the credit or get paid for it."

"Oh wow."

"Yeah, it was really shitty. But people still talk about it."

"Oh yeah?"

"Yes, there's a fan club out there for 'Barkingly Ever After.' Look it up on Reddit sometime if you want to have a laugh. It's actually quite touching to see how much people identified with it."

"That's great."

"It's sweet. I gave up the business after that. I still think about getting back in it some days."

"That's good. You should get back in it." I didn't know what else to say.

A personal reminder that I too had been chewed up by the business but not quite spit out. And another person I'm supposed to hold space for and make feel OK in the moment.

I don't know what it's like to not get credit for a script you wrote, but I do know what it's like to pose on a red carpet for three years while your costar makes ten times what you do not including other monies from being exec. producer and getting back end.

This guy was assuming a random stranger (me) who is a woman would be willing to stand and listen to his sad story about how he wasn't appreciated while he boasted about how talented he thought he was.

I catch myself thinking I should have more than I do, then I remember that the super rich are the saddest of all because they have the number-one spot, but when they pull that sports car into their six-car garage after an exhilarating Sunday-morning drive, there's still space. As they close the car door and walk toward their massive house, there's still a "What do I do next?" feeling.

The pandemic has been a spotlight accelerating the necessity to come to terms with who I really am. Not a superstar with a glamorous lifestyle, but a divorced parent with diminishing returns of a career in acting trying to keep it all together and hoping for a job in show business. Now, like a drunk without a drink, I have all of this space that needs filling.

At this point, one of the drunk guys followed me into the *lavandería* and sat down on the bench while he spoke in Spanish. I was taking an Instagram story of the items in the vending machines while he stared at me. He was very drunk but seemed nice and jolly, so when I realized he was talking to me I gave him a glance, smile, and a nod. That seemed to get him going. He tried broken English to me and said: "You eat *frutas*?" I eat *frutas*? He wants to know if I eat fruit.

"I do."

"*Frutas* and *vegetales*."

I smiled. "Yes, I eat fruits and vegetables."

"You a stronga mama." I looked deep into his wobbly eyes.

"Yes. I am a strong mama." I think he was looking at my legs and ass in my spandex but I took it to mean: I'm a strong mama who can do anything. Then I got into my car and cried.

Back at the cozy cottage I went to take a shower and the water came up to my ankles and wouldn't drain. Fine. I get it. My life is at a standstill. So I'll deal with it. I'll enjoy my alone time while being profoundly disappointed that I am no longer home base. Dad's weird condo is now the familiar place where my son has his own room with his basketball poster on the wall and the quilt his grandma made for him. I'm flailing in a cozy cottage with uneven crusty walls and four broken can openers and an oven that doesn't work. OK, then, I won't open cans or use the oven. And now, to avoid getting runoff dirty water up to my ankles in the shower, I wash my hair in the sink before taking a shower. I name the cockroaches and compare their sizes and frequency of appearance as I wonder what my son is doing with his dad. And what my son and his dad are doing without me while I prepare to start over. Again. I am a strong mama.

# HOW NOT TO DATE AFTER A DIVORCE

1. Don't join a celebrity dating app.

There was a vetting process to promote their exclusivity. Emotionally, I was already raw; it took two months for the site to decide I was good enough to pay them to show me potential love partners. This just might be the thing that puts me over the edge. When I finally got on, there was a real shortage of celebrities.

One guy (not a celebrity) who I had distanced myself from and didn't want to date in real life found me. "Hey, I didn't know you were on this app!"

The other thing about the app was they chose how many people you were allowed to see. You couldn't browse too much. They would say, "That's enough for today! Enjoy the group of people you have already browsed in our community." Oh I'm sorry, I didn't realize I was part of a community. Finally, after a half-dozen rounds, their algorithm showed me the goods: Owen Wilson, Matt LeBlanc, Chris Rock. Of course, I hit "like" on all of them. I knew none would respond and that I wouldn't want to date them anyway. But I had to know.

Actually, there was one other person who clicked on me. A tech mogul from Marin County. He and I talked on the phone. He told me he did long mountain bike rides. Spandex and mountain bikes? I'm out.

Then someone got matched with me. It was an ex-boyfriend. So now I was paying this app to outright troll me? Got it. But I was open to it. *Maybe I need to be open to giving this another chance. I loved him before, and we've both grown . . . and the app thinks we're a good match. Besides it would be so much nicer than having to meet someone new and start over completely.*

2. Don't go out with the ex-boyfriend you matched with on the app. He invited me over. When I saw him at the door it was sweet. It felt warm and familiar but new again. Not a high-risk mystery or a horny excitement. We shared a hug. He cooked steak and baked potatoes. He made the entire bag of potatoes—I'm not sure why. We talked about our divorces and people from the past we have in common. We drank sake.

After dinner, we went to sit in the front room. There was a big heavy coffee table in the living room. Huge and made out of thick wood. "It is the door of a ship," he said. There was no room to sit on the couch without running into the ship door table.

"Oh . . ." I had to act fast and bring my legs up onto the couch, taking a yoga pose, as there was no room for me to have my feet on the floor. This unconscious choice of his, even in the moment of a person actively trying to sit down, still went unnoticed by him.

"I got it from David Crosby's son."

"Crosby, Stills, and Nash?"

"I want to sell it. It's worth twenty-six hundred dollars."

"No one is going to pay twenty-sex hundred dollars. You need to take a few hundred for it and call it a day."

"I looked it up, I'll show you where it says twenty-six hundred."

"It's not going to happen." He was subconsciously saying, *I don't want anyone to sit on this couch with me.* There was no room for me there, no matter what he said. I was convinced that was his way of psychically telling me to get out and so I did.

3. Don't go out with another ex.

I also got a long text from another ex, Carlo, the one I broke up with fifteen years ago in an alley where there was a dead rat. Yes, that's the second dead rat to be mentioned in this book, if you're keeping score.

"Let me make dinner for you. Come to my place so I can cook for you." He decorated his place for the date, quaint fake candles everywhere. Yellow flowers for me (I don't like yellow flowers). I couldn't appreciate his effort. I kept saying, "Thank you," and, "This is amazing," but I didn't want any of it. I was distracted because I was in the middle of selling my house to get the cash out and downsizing to a condo.

I apologized for getting up to check my phone every couple of minutes and then talking to my real estate agents during the third course. I tried to make light of it and include him, telling him how much I loved my real estate agents, a husband-and-wife team. I showed him a picture of the husband's headshot. He had a very large porn mustache.

The date felt false to me. I got physical with him anyway, hoping that would feel better. It didn't. He didn't seem to notice. He texted me five days later.

"Come to NYC. I'll fly you."

"Haha," I replied.

"We don't have to sleep in the same bed," he wrote. That was the least of my concerns. I couldn't leave all of my responsibilities and go to New York. For him, it was freeing and fun. For me, it sounded like a nightmare. He didn't understand anything about my life. I don't pick up and go across the country with no notice. I have a child, an ex, and pets. I'm also in the middle of moving. How could he be so unaware and how did I not see this years ago?

4. Don't spend too much time thinking about getting back together with your ex-husband.

I saw this video online that was captured by a Ring camera. The wife was headed to the car, carrying a bunch of stuff. She was a few steps away from the car door when a small animal, visible in the lower left of the screen, runs after her. At first you think it must be a dog. But it's too muscular and the movement is too fast. It was a rabid mountain lion! The bottom half of the woman's body is obscured by the parked car, and the next thing you see, what you assume, is the animal clamping on to the back of her legs and the woman lurching to the ground, her stuff flying everywhere. On the other side of the screen, the husband has entered the picture carrying a tray of cupcakes. He drops his tray, runs over to his wife, and grabs the mountain lion. He swings it in the air and throws it off of her kicking at it as it hits the ground.

I thought, *It would be really nice to have a husband in a time like this. Maybe I made a mistake. I don't have a man by my side to protect me from nature's predators. I might not need him for the everyday moments when he doesn't talk or even really want to be in*

*the same room with me. But to have him around in case of a rabid*
*mountain lion attack, it might be worth it.*

It's scary to be by yourself. It's comforting to have a partner. But sometimes the dangers outweigh the comfort. If you have thoughts like this about your ex-husband, or any circumstance in your life that you wish you could go back to, just wait it out. It will pass. Also, I believe I could punch and throw a mountain lion, if necessary.

.

# LOOKING FOR LOVE IN ALL THE WRONG PLACES

During the pandemic, the closest I came to dating was watching CNN while eating and then telling people I had dinner with Don Lemon. "I really had to be there for Don tonight. He was so upset about Trump, he couldn't even speak."

Then there was a stunning turn of events. It was a hundred degrees Fahrenheit and I was running what I like to call the mother lode of errands deep in the San Fernando Valley: laundry, breakfast, and the pet store. I put the laundry in, then hit 7-Eleven for a protein cookie and a drink. I luxuriated while my clothes were in the washer. Then, when it was time for the dryer, I hit the pet store. On my way back as I was lifting the fifty-pound bag of food into the back of my car, a guy drove by in a big black GMC truck, rolled his window down and said, "Hi!" He waved.

I waved back. "Hi!" He drove by and I finished putting my pet supplies in the car. As I was walking back into the laundromat to get my clothes, he circled back by me, driving really slow, with his window down again. "Hey . . ."

I stopped and turned around. "Hey," I said.

"I wanted to say hi to you . . ."

"Oh, OK."

"It was so nice that you said hi back. Most people don't do that." Wait. What? Is he flirting with me? Little ol' forty-nine-year-old me in my palm tree spandex leggings and bedazzled slides from Skechers. My hair was dirty and unbrushed and I had no makeup on and I still got it. Hell yeah. My ass must have been working overtime.

"Oh really, people don't say hi?!" I threw it back to him to see if he had a better line.

"You've been doing laundry for a long time." Nope. In fact, that was a borderline creepy thing to say.

"Yeah . . ."

"I drove by here earlier and saw you and I came back and you're still here."

"Oh, really?" Is it sexy or stalking if someone keeps driving past where you are? Then he follows all that up with this stunner.

"Yeah, I was at the grocery store getting my car registration. Did you know they have a machine where you can do that?" A guy with hot tips on how to get your car registered, yes, please!

"Wow, that's cool."

"You get it out of a machine. Look, I got the sticker!" He tested me on BLM, asking subtly if I went to a march. Testing to see if I was a Trumpy. Then he dropped that he's former military. Ooh la la. His name was John and he asked if he could give me his number. He then asked me if I would take my mask down—he'd like to see my face. I complied. Other than his boldness and being former military, he seemed straight, normal, and responsible. Maybe this is exactly what I needed.

I texted him hello later that day. It was basic. "What are you doing?" he asked. Somehow I didn't get that he was asking what I was doing right then. I thought he meant in life, so when he asked if I wanted to meet for coffee in an hour, I was surprised. We sat outdoors on a Starbucks patio with our masks on.

I didn't have my lie prepared so I told him I did comedy. When I said that he looked me up and down.

"Tell me a joke." This is the last thing a comic ever wants to hear.

"No . . ." He wasn't perceptive. He tried to coax me. He said he would get me out of my shell. I kept telling him I wasn't going to do that. Until I finally said, "That's not how it works. The more you ask, the less I feel like talking. Besides, I get paid to tell jokes."

"Oh, well I didn't mean to offend you."

"It's not offensive." I'm a professional comedian, maybe I should have a story at the ready. Mostly, I was really not into being asked about being funny by someone not funny at all.

He asked me, "What type of things do you like to do?"

"Um I like to go on walks, stare at my animals. Watch TV I guess."

"Do you like wine?"

"Yes."

"We could go to wine country. We could drive to Santa Barbara."

*Dude, I don't know you.*

"That sounds really nice." Sometimes I say what people want to hear just to keep it going. He started showing me pictures of his kids and saying how we could watch movies and go to concerts. He wanted me to know he was serious. He doesn't date around.

"Do you?"

"Do I what?"

"Date around?"

"No, I mean I've talked with a couple of my exes."

"I'm looking for a companion, like I don't want to be seeing a bunch of people."

"Me neither."

"Do you like me?"

"Yeah . . ." *How can I say no to his face?*

"You don't have to have walls up. Here, give me a hug." We hugged and then I turned away. "What's your rush?"

"Nothing I guess."

*Is this how people act?* I was turned off by his agenda, which apparently was to have an instant relationship. He was physically attractive but I couldn't get over the "Tell me a joke" thing. We couldn't move on to exclusivity on the first date *after* he completely misjudged me and didn't understand anything about me.

"OK, well you know, just relax. See if you like me."

"You're a good-looking guy."

"Really? Why do you have walls up?"

"I don't. I just gotta go."

"Do you like Italian food? I can take you to the best Italian food on Wednesday."

"Sure. See you later." I texted him two hours later that not only can I not get Italian food, but also I cannot speak to him again.

I needed to try to date someone who wasn't so far out of my realm. Someone who knows I'm an actor and comedian and doesn't ask me to tell them a joke (but would laugh at a joke).

To my surprise, I would meet someone with those qualifications about a week later. He was a stranger but he was a friend of a friend. We were both actors. We acted together in a shoot outdoors during

COVID. When we met, he said he knew me but I didn't remember him. He reminded me that we met more than once. I tried to not beat myself up for not remembering. I told myself: *It's OK that he remembers you and you don't remember him—you're an international superstar.*

He was humble and gentle yet strong. He was funny and present. He seemed mature and intelligent. I let his first impression be magnificent. Like the show *Married at First Sight*, which I had been watching a lot when I wasn't having dinner with Don Lemon. When they meet, it's magical because both people project onto the other what they want to see.

I asked my friend who was directing the shoot we did together for his number. I texted him. He didn't respond right away. When he did, it was like a riddle: "I'd like to sit by a pool and drink a cocktail with you." So he is interested.

I wrote back that I would like that and he didn't respond. I had just watched *The Social Dilemma*, so I thought he showed more positive phone habits than the normal person who you would think would be texting back right away. *He is not constantly on his phone. How refreshing! This will fit in with my new lifestyle of getting out of the matrix of social media. We won't need our phones because we'll be together!*

A couple of days into the chat, he said he realized that he can't let any more time pass and locked down a date with me. Now we're talking! He recognized that I am a queen.

He told me to meet him in Malibu for a picnic. I approved.

He said he was going to stop at a fancy grocery store and get some salads. I was loving this guy's ideas! I would also stop at the fancy grocery store. I got butternut squash, sriracha chicken wings, and watermelon. I wanted to get items that would complement whatever main courses he was going to bring. I was going to bring a blanket but I didn't want to take over the situation—I wanted to follow his lead.

I pulled up when the date was supposed to start. I received a text. Not before he was late, but as he was being late. The text read "I'm seventeen minutes out." *Bitch, the date already started! Why didn't you text me seventeen minutes ago*?! Then I thought maybe his perception of time is different from mine.

He walked up with a small, lunch-bag-size cooler strapped to his shoulder. I'm wondering how he fit our gourmet grocery store spread in such a small container. Maybe it's like a Mary Poppins carpet bag: He'll pull out flowers, champagne, and some puppies. We walked around looking for a place to sit in the blazing sun. Each patch of shade or bench was already occupied. Our only option was a bumpy, dirty area under a little tree.

"You didn't bring a blanket? Me either!" I laughed but it wasn't funny. "I stopped at three grocery stores, but there were lines." *Yeah, no shit there's lines, it's a pandemic.* He pulled out a sandwich from Subway. I pulled out my food and he said, "Healthy!" *You mean, normal?!*

He mumbled and gestured with his Subway sandwich. Was he trying to offer me some? He laughed. I laughed too. I think Subway is disgusting but I couldn't say that. *That's how he eats! Who am I to judge? But what happened to the fancy grocery store idea that he had? Stop being a bitch and just go with the flow. Do I want to be right or do I want to be happy?* He then asked if I got a babysitter to be on this date.

"No, my son is with his dad." It felt like a weird breech. *He doesn't know about babysitters or kids or my kid or my life. I could not imagine him ever meeting my child.* I pushed that thought down. I responded as if he were a regular adult.

"Yeah, I'm staying at this Airbnb right now because I had to sell my house to get the equity out, and my son doesn't want to sleep there. It's weird not being home base anymore." Crickets. After we finished our meal, him eating his sandwich, me eating the bounty I had brought, we went for a walk. He seemed to be moving really slow on flat ground. He then mentioned that if I see him limping, it's because he aggravated his torn meniscus.

"You have a torn meniscus right now?"

"Yeah."

"Isn't that painful?"

"Yeah, usually I would take a cane."

"Oh."

"Yeah, I injured it ten years ago. I was supposed to get surgery, but my friend who is a doctor told me to wait because of medical advancements they're making."

"You have had this for ten years?!" This was reasonable to him.

He went on to tell an anecdote about how he acted in a scene with Samuel L. Jackson a decade ago, wherein he had one line but then tried to talk to Samuel L. Jackson about his character's motivation and was ignored. I think this was the only movie he had been in. He was trying to relate to me as a fellow professional actor. I felt a pressure to respond excitedly or with some level of investment. It was uncomfortable. Then I remembered I'm an actual movie star. How does the sun relate to a speck of sand?

*He wants me to think he's a big deal.* So I let him talk. Besides, if I gave my acting anecdotes this date would be three days long.

Then we saw a couple and the guy was in a football jersey.

"Yeah, I could be watching football but I'm here with you." *Oh, how sweet.*

"*You* picked this date and time."

"I'm just saying . . ." I still told myself I shouldn't judge him, he's just a straight guy.

We sat on a bench. I wasn't expecting it, but he went in for a kiss. It was like a side-cheek kiss that brushed the side of my face. I was starving for physical affection and since my theme of the day was to shove my actual feelings down to make him feel better about himself, I went with it. Besides, what better time to make out with a stranger than during a pandemic.

I was going through the motions and waiting for my body to kick in. Waiting for my sexual feelings to show their head. I drummed up a small flicker but mostly was faking it. I let him think the date was a success as I tried to convince myself it was.

At two A.M. I woke up in a rage remembering this: He brought one Subway sandwich. *This motherfucker brought one Subway sandwich! And he also told me an anal sex joke! Why?* What is wrong with me that I wanted to make everything OK above all else to the point that I'm just now putting it together that he brought a single Subway sandwich, one bag of chips, and one cookie?! And you know he didn't say "light mayo" when he ordered the turkey sandwich. You know that the sandwich artist at Subway is going to put an overly liberal amount of mayonnaise on there. Every way you look at it, this scenario is not how a lady wants to be treated.

So you didn't make it to the gourmet grocery store, you're at Subway. At the very least get two sandwiches, since there's two people. Then you get ALL of the chips. You get every single kind of chip and you give me my choice. It's a date. I don't know you. And you get every cookie and allow me to pick. You're at Subway! You should buy me the entire store and treat me like the queen that I am. Who shows up with one sandwich?!

I can't blame him. I attracted a one-sandwich guy and agreed to go out with him without assessing the situation and without standing up for myself. This highlights my need to people please and say yes because I'm so flattered that anyone would ask me out. This behavior is so deeply ingrained in me that I'm not sure how to break it. The next time I say yes to a date after careful consideration and someone brings only one sandwich, I've got to yell "No!" and slap the sandwich out of his dirty hand and stomp on it. "No!" as I bring my knee up quickly into his nuts. I learned this in my self-defense for ladies class. How could I have forgotten?

# A STAR IS BORN

When I travel away from my home to other places, it gets me thinking about the big picture. Then, returning home from a trip, I'll assess if I'm where I want to be in my life. One time, I was driving home from the airport, sitting on the freeway on a gray day in Los Angeles, and it hit me that I was too old to be a young mother. I called my mom, crying, and said, "I'm too old to be a young mother." She told me I had plenty of time if I really wanted to be a mom.

Six years later, I was actually pregnant but my mom didn't know. I didn't want to tell her—I was afraid of how she and my dad would react. I wasn't married and they had not met the guy who got me pregnant.

When I visited my parents in Michigan that Christmas, I knew I was pregnant and I had to tell them. I hadn't been seeing him very long and he was not settled in his life. He lived in his friend's house rent free and was without a job, wanting to be an actor. But we were in love and had agreed to give it a go as a family. This was the only ammunition I had. I waited until I was on my way out the door to the airport before I told them. I had my backpack and my suitcase, had said my goodbyes and I love yous, and turned around to tell them. I mustered up the courage and through pursed lips with an apologetic tone I said, "Mom, Dad, something happened." I felt sick. My dad was facing the television and sighed deeply, so I knew I had his attention. My mother looked terrified, bracing for the worst. "I'm pregnant." My mom jumped up, gave me a high-five and a huge hug. "I'm so happy for you," she said.

"You are?"

"Yes! I didn't think you were going to do it and that would be fine too, but I'm so happy for you!" That's when I realized, *Oh, I'm thirty-six years old and I can make my own life decisions.* She went on, "You can do this!"

"Yes, well Matt and I decided we are going to do it together."

"You don't need him. If it works, that's nice but you don't need him." What she meant was, *You have TV money, you're set for life, you're Chloe O'Brian! Also, I don't trust men!*

When I got back to LA, it was time to start going to doctors' appointments. Our first one was pretty harrowing. A nurse sat us down with an exhaustive list of questions. "OK, let's get started. I have here a list of medical questions, answer to the best of your abilities."

"OK."

"We'll start with you, Mary Lynn. Have you or anyone in your family had cancer?" Wow! That's a loaded question.

"Yeah I'd rather not say!"

"Diabetes?"

"No."

"Stroke?"

"Nope!"

"Cystic fibrosis?"

It went on like this for a while until it got to my favorite part (besides do we do drugs or have mental disorders), which was "Have you slept with anyone you're related to?" *No, and I don't understand how this could affect my unborn child!* And then I figured out she wanted to know if our child would be inbred.

His answer was no as well. Whew, I mean I assumed he hadn't but I guess you never know! There is so much faith put under the general heading of "This guy is cool." We make all kinds of assumptions about each other when we are attracted to them and get along, but this interview with the nurse made me realize that it's not a bad idea to ask someone on a first date if they ever had sex with their cousin. It's good information to know!

The appointments at the beginning were all the same. I picked the first ob-gyn on the list that my insurance provided, Dr. Abini. That was the extent of the vetting process. Every week I would go and he'd say, "There's the baby's heartbeat. Any questions for me?"

"Nope." Then we'd be on our way. Next week, same thing. "There's the heartbeat, do you have any questions?"

"Nope." Week after week, until two weeks before my due date. "There's the heartbeat, do you have any—oh hey, I just remembered I'm going to be out of town on your due date, if you'd like to schedule a C-section for this week." Wha?! We never talked about this! I told him I'd think about it. Then, in the parking lot I was incensed. "C-section?! What is he talking about? What about my baby and my body? I want to do it naturally?! How dare he!" I was not ready to hear that.

So we fired him and hired a doula. She told us all kinds of things that Mr. Ob-gyn didn't want us to know. Like, did you know that you don't need harmful drugs to have a baby? Turns out all you need is a little tree sap. Nature's antiseptic. And do you know how women used to induce labor in the old days? Square dancing! Hmm, do I want to be strapped to a stainless-steel table in a hospital being shot full of drugs or square dancing in a field? Tough call, Mr. Ob-gyn, Mr. Man, up in your hospital! Then I watched this documentary by Ricki Lake and this woman had her baby in a creek! She sighs and the baby slips right out into the water! Sign me up for that. "Swing your partner round and round, tree sap tree sap, baby come on down." This is going to be fun.

It was fun, for a while. I started my contractions in a park leaning up against a tree when a passerby asked if I was OK. "Yep, managing a couple of contractions here. No problem. Nice weather we're having. Hello, squirrel!" I went home, got my baby boudoir all set up with the candles, the Stevie Wonder compact discs, and most important, the inflatable pool with warm water. I felt serene, it was time to have a baby! The next couple of hours were really nice. Then it was time for the doulas to arrive. The contractions were getting closer together and more painful as the sun started to go down. The whole thing was going faster now. Harder, painful, took a lot of focus. But we were all managing. I was having contractions every couple of minutes and also changing positions. Lying on the bed, squatting, on the toilet, in the pool, out of the pool. At one point, I wandered into the kitchen where a junior assistant doula was sitting on my kitchen floor looking at her phone. She looked up, saw me, and said, "Have you ever really cried?" I stared at her, then went back into the bedroom.

I had been in labor since eleven A.M., it was eleven P.M. and it was definitely not fun anymore. One of the doulas said, "You should feel like you're having a bowel movement and push from there. Your water will be breaking any minute." The momentum came and went. My water never broke and no one said anything. The contractions were terrible. I was in so much pain, I couldn't focus on anything else. I was walking around like an angry bull, my baby daddy tried to put a bite of banana in my mouth. I spit it out. I passed out on the bed. I woke up for each contraction literally trying to scratch that white witch's eyes out. The baby had stopped advancing down the birth canal and I continued to have contractions. I was passed out from pain and we were at a standstill. It was now a nightmare.

Finally, around nine the next morning, my heroic boyfriend called it. He said he had made a decision and we needed to go to the hospital. The doulas' hospital of choice, which we went along with, was Cedars-Sinai, a hospital known by name to be the favorite of the rich and famous. It was also an hour away in rush hour traffic. Again, my soon-to-be husband stepped in and made the decision to go back to the hospital of the ob-gyn we had fired, which was four minutes away.

When we got to the emergency room, we were no longer registered at the hospital for the birth. We begged our way in. It didn't hurt that one of the nurses recognized me, although she did say, "Why don't you call Jack Bauer to help!" Luckily, Dr. Abini was available to come and deliver the baby, who was two weeks past his due date. The doulas followed us up to the room. I was told that I would still be able to get an epidural. A doula came over to whisper in my ear, "You can still try for natural. We'll advocate for you."

Suddenly, I found my voice loud and clear: "I WANT THE EPI-DURAL, NOW!" Dr. Abini came in and informed us that the baby's heart rate was dropping and he wanted to do a C-section. Again, the doula came to ask me if I wanted to try natural. Dr. Abini said, out loud, while the baby was still inside of me, "This is why I don't like home births—I've delivered too many dead babies." Wow. Mic drop. Whut. Talk about bringing down the room.

We were in the operating room within ten minutes. Within thirty minutes, our son was born via C-section. I was on drugs in a twilight state and before I knew it Matt was holding our son. I stared at the two of them and asked, "Is this the baby?" It was. I wasn't so sure about it at first, but it didn't take long until I realized automatically that I would do anything for this child. There would be no hesitation to push him out of the way of the bus and take the hit myself. Having this baby was the best thing both of us ever did and ever will do.

We asked Dr. Abini to circumcise him. I didn't know enough about not circumcising and besides I couldn't imagine cleaning all around the penis folds. Oh, the baby was a boy, I forgot to say that. We thanked Dr. Abini for saving both of our lives. I thanked Matt for making the call. I never talked to those doulas again. I have cried a lot but I don't know if I "really cried" the way the junior assistant doula meant. I will never know what the fuck she was talking about.

# ACKNOWLEDGMENTS

Thank you to Dan Dion at 800lb Gorilla for introducing me to my book agent, Peter McGuigan, at Ultra Literary (brilliant and devastatingly handsome in a rugged, blue-collar kind of way would be too long to include), who made this all so easy to get off the ground. Thank you to the publishers who turned me down so that I could work with the wonderful Samantha Weiner and the entire Abrams team: Annalea Manalili, Devin Grosz, Diane Shaw, Jen Brunn, Gabby Fisher, and Mamie VanLangen. Thank you to Stacy Creamer for jumping aboard this project with such joy and enthusiasm, and the whole team at Audible: Jeff Golick, Mallaigh Nolan, and Kathrin Lambrix. Thank you, Itay Reiss for always helping out when I call on you. God bless the team proofreading the actor/comic's memoirs who came in with comments like, "I knew this information the first couple of times you said it, no need to restate." I appreciate your world-weary candor at my repeats and slang way of speaking. You went through it all and that could not have been easy. As a comic on stage, we repeat things to keep the attention of drunk audiences. I wager a bet that some people will be drunk reading my book, so I stand behind anything and everything over-stated. For anything underwritten, I'd like to acknowledge that, as an actor, I say words that are written for me, and sometimes you have to look at my face and hear my tone to understand context. If you are unsure while reading, may I advise to please refer to the cover of the book and imagine that person saying the words.

Special thanks to my ex-husband, Matt, who doesn't complain as I mine our relationship, marriage, and divorce over and over for material.

To my son, Valentine, the light of my life. I love fighting with you.

Zach Kleiman, for helping me to see there are things to believe in.

Special thanks to Chelsea Mitchell for being with me every step of the way. There was no shortage of blankets, candles, and incense in the making of this book. Thank you, Chelsea, for believing in me, listening to me, laughing at me, and "making space," as they say, for this book to be written. We worked through my divorce, selling my house, and my dog dying. I am forever grateful.

To Leo and Dikembe, for your companionship, troublemaking, nonstop entertainment, and cuddles, thank you.